Collins

KS3
Geography
Revision Guide

David Rayner, Andrew Browne, Victoria Turner, Adam Gibson and Tony Grundy

About this Revision & Practice book

When it comes to getting the best results, practice really does make perfect! Experts have proved that repeatedly testing yourself on a topic is far more effective than re-reading information over and over again. And, to be as effective as possible, you should space out the practice test sessions over time. This Complete Revision & Practice book is specially designed to support this approach to revision and includes seven different opportunities to test yourself on each topic, spaced out over time.

Revise

These pages provide a recap of everything you need to know for each topic. All key words are defined in the glossary.

You should read through all the information before taking the Quick Test at the end. This will test whether you can recall the key facts.

> **Quick Test**
>
> 1. What type of environmental region covers most of Russia?
> 2. What is the frozen ground found in tundra regions known as?
> 3. Name Russia's most economically important river.
> 4. What is the population of Russia's second largest city?

Practise

These topic-based questions appear shortly after the revision pages for each topic and will test whether you have understood the topic. If you get any of the questions wrong, make sure you read the correct answer carefully.

Review

These topic-based questions appear later in the book, allowing you to revisit the topic and test how well you have remembered the information. If you get any of the questions wrong, make sure you read the correct answer carefully.

Mix it Up

These pages feature a mix of questions for all the different topics, just like you would get in a test.

Test Yourself on the Go

Visit our website at **collins.co.uk/collinsks3revision** and print off a set of flashcards. These pocket-sized cards feature questions and answers so that you can test yourself on all the key facts anytime and anywhere. You will also find lots more information about the advantages of spaced practice and how to plan for it.

Workbook

This section features even more topic-based questions as well as mixed test-style questions, providing two further practice opportunities for each topic to guarantee the best results.

ebook

To access the ebook, visit **collins.co.uk/ebooks** and follow the step-by-step instructions.

QR Codes

Found throughout the book, the QR codes can be scanned on your smartphone for extra practice and explanations.

A QR code in the Revise section links to a Quick Recall Quiz on that topic. A QR code in the Workbook section links to a video working through the solution to one of the questions on that topic.

Contents

Review Questions

Key Concepts from Key Stage 2

World Geography

1

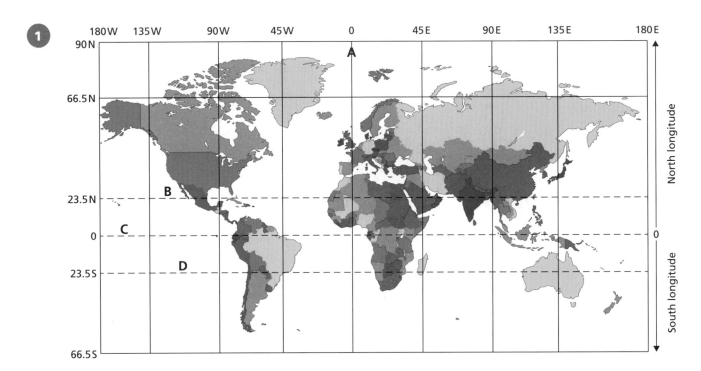

a) Complete the table below by writing the letter from the map next to the correct name of the line in the table.

Equator	
Tropic of Capricorn	
Tropic of Cancer	
Greenwich Meridian	

[4]

b) Which colour are the following countries on the world map?

   i) Brazil   **ii)** Argentina   **iii)** Italy   **iv)** USA   **v)** Sweden   [5]

Physical Geography

2 **a)** **i)** Name the scale that is used to measure the magnitude of an earthquake.   [1]

   ii) What is the word for the point on the ground surface above where an earthquake happens?   [1]

   iii) What is the word for a volcano that is never going to erupt again?   [1]

b) **i)** Match the words below to the correct labels on the diagram of a river system.

Tributary   Confluence   Watershed   Mouth   Source

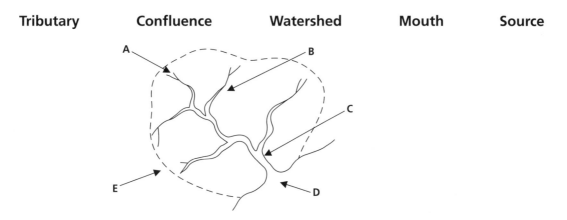

[5]

ii) Describe how the water cycle works by using the words below to fill in the gaps.

throughflow   evaporation   run-off   precipitation   condensation

The Sun heats the sea, which causes .... Water vapour rises into the sky

and as it cools .... takes place to form clouds. The water droplets fall as

rain, snow or hail, also known as .... The water flows back to the sea in

streams and rivers and overland as .... , through soil as ....

and through bedrock as groundwater flow. [5]

Human Geography

3 **a)** Match each type of economic activity with the correct occupation.

Primary activity	Dentist
Secondary activity	Farmer
Tertiary activity	Programmer
Quaternary activity	Metal worker

[4]

b) Choose the correct settlement types from the pair of choices in the sentences below.

i) Most **towns/cities** in the UK have a cathedral, hospital and university. [1]

ii) A **village/hamlet** is a rural settlement with a small population that is unlikely to have a church or primary school. [1]

iii) A region where a number of urban areas have grown together is known as a **city/conurbation**. [1]

Location Knowledge – Russia

Quick Recall Quiz

You must be able to:

- Describe the environmental regions of Russia
- Understand the key physical and human characteristics of Russia
- Name the major cities of Russia.

Environmental Regions

- **Tundra** is found in the far north of Russia. Temperatures can fall to as low as −50°C in the winter. Trees cannot grow because it is too cold and the ground is frozen all year round (**permafrost**).
- **Taiga** is a region of coniferous trees such as pine, spruce and fir that covers approximately 60% of Russia.
- **Steppe** is a region of grassland plains south of the taiga. The climate is too dry for forests to grow but the soil, known as **chernozem**, is very fertile and good for agriculture.
- **Semi-arid** deserts are located in the far south of Russia where summer temperatures can reach over 38°C and total annual rainfall is less than 250 mm.
- **Deciduous** forests containing oak, ash, birch and beech trees are found in the west of Russia.

> **Key Point**
>
> All of the major climate zones can be found in Russia, apart from tropical.

Physical and Human Characteristics

- Russia is the largest country in the world. It is 1.8 times larger than the USA and covers over 17 million km^2.
- Economically, Russia's most important river is the Volga, which is 3692 km long (making it Europe's longest river).
- The Urals mountain range runs north to south across Western Russia. It creates a boundary between European Russia and Siberia, a region consisting mainly of cold steppe and tundra covering 77% of Russia.
- Russia's highest mountain is Mt Elbrus (5642 m) in the Caucasus Mountains, which mark the border between Southern Russia and Georgia.
- Russia has many **natural resources** including natural gas, oil, coal, iron ore, timber and gold. The total potential value of Russia's resources is estimated to be $30 trillion.
- There are 15 cities in Russia with a population of 1 million or more. The capital of Russia is Moscow, which has a population of 12.5 million (2022). Russia's second city is St Petersburg with a population of 5.5 million (2022).
- The population of Russia declined from 149 million in 1991 to 142.7 million in 2008, and by 2021 had slowly recovered to 146 million.

Tundra

Taiga

- Following the collapse of the Soviet Union in 1991, the uncertain future of their country made Russians reluctant to have large families.
- Russia has the 11th largest economy in the world. Its main industries are in manufacturing, such as defence and motor vehicles. High-tech industries, including information technology, nanotechnology and the space industry, are growing rapidly.
- Vladimir Putin was president from 2000–2008 and was re-elected in 2012. From 2000 to 2010, the economy grew rapidly at an average of 7% each year, but growth has slowed since 2010 to 1.3% in 2019. People's incomes have doubled and the proportion of the population living in poverty has been significantly reduced.
- In 2014 Russia hosted the Winter Olympics in Sochi, on the north-east coast of the Black Sea. It cost Russia $51 billion to stage, making it the most expensive Olympic Games in history. Russia also hosted the football World Cup in 2018 and held Formula 1 Grand Prix races at Sochi until the country's invasion of Ukraine in 2022.

Development Indicators for Russia	
Gross Domestic Product (GDP) (per capita)	$12 172 (2021)
Employment structure	Primary 6%; Secondary 27%; Tertiary & Quaternary 67%
Life expectancy	73 years
Literacy rate	Male: 99.7%; Female 99.7% (2019)
Human Development Index (HDI)	0.824 (52nd out of 189 countries, in 2020)
Individuals using the Internet	85% of total population (2020)
Renewable energy consumption	3.2% of total energy consumption (2019)

Moscow

Steppe

> **Key Point**
>
> Today, even though the economy is growing, rising childcare costs and a desire to concentrate on their careers mean people are still choosing to have fewer children.

> **Key Words**
>
> tundra
> permafrost
> taiga
> steppe
> chernozem
> semi-arid
> deciduous
> natural resources

Quick Test

1. What type of environmental region covers most of Russia?
2. What is the frozen ground found in tundra regions known as?
3. Name Russia's most economically important river.
4. What is the population of Russia's second largest city?

Location Knowledge – China

Quick Recall Quiz

You must be able to:

- Describe the environmental regions of China
- Understand the key physical and human characteristics of China
- Name the major cities of China.

Environmental Regions

- Taiga (coniferous forests) and steppe (grasslands) are found in north-east China including the Manchurian Plain, which covers an area of 350 000 km^2.
- The North China Plain is a lowland area in eastern China that covers an area of 409 500 km^2. Here there is a **sub-tropical** monsoon climate with cold, dry winters and hot, wet summers. This is a major agricultural region where wheat, cotton, peanuts, tea, rice and tobacco are grown.
- **Tropical rainforest** is found in south-east China. On Hainan Island, China's southern-most point, over 3000 species of plants and more than 4700 species of animal have been recorded.
- North-west China contains two major **cold deserts**, the Gobi Desert and the Taklamakan Desert. The Gobi Desert is 1.3 million km^2, temperatures can vary from as low as –40°C to as high as 40°C and it receives an average of 194 mm of precipitation a year (some of it falling as snow).
- The Tibetan Plateau is in south-west China. It is over 4500 m above sea level and covers 2.5 million km^2 (four times the area of France). It is an area of **alpine tundra** characterised by grasses and low shrubs, with wildlife such as bears, marmots and yak.

Physical and Human Characteristics

- China is the third largest country in the world covering an area of 9.6 million km^2.
- The longest river in China is the Yangtze. It is 6300 km long, making it the third longest river in the world after the Nile and the Amazon.
- China has 1500 rivers that drain **catchment areas** of over 1000 km^2.
- North and north-west China are in a major **earthquake** zone; on 12 May 2008 the Sichuan earthquake struck. At 8 on the **Richter scale**, it was the 21st deadliest earthquake ever recorded; 87 000 were killed and 374 000 injured.
- China has the largest population in the world, with approximately 1.41 billion in 2021.

Key Point

Mt Everest, the tallest mountain in the world at 8849 m, is located on the China-Nepal border.

Rice farming

One Child Policy

China's **One Child Policy** ran from 1979 to 2015. Due to its success, reducing the number of births by an estimated 400 million, it was relaxed in 2015 to allow two children per couple. It was changed again to allow three children, which many saw as a good thing. Whilst the policy prevented overpopulation, it was unpopular with a lot of Chinese people.

- There are over 600 cities in China and more than 150 of these have a population of at least a million:
  - The largest city in China is Shanghai (28.5 million in 2022)
  - The capital, Beijing, has 21.5 million
  - Chongqing has 16.9 million (2022).
- China is the world's second largest economy, after the USA. Dominated by **manufacturing** and construction, China's economy has been growing at an average rate of about 6.5% since 2015.
- China is a **Communist** country with only one political party, the Communist Party. The government used to own and control all the agriculture and industry, but since 1978 the government has allowed people to own and run their own businesses.

Development Indicators for China	
Gross Domestic Product (GDP) (per capita)	$10 430
Employment structure	Primary 24%; Secondary 29%; Tertiary & Quaternary 47%
Life expectancy	77 years
Literacy rate	Male: 98.5%; Female 95.2% (2019)
Human Development Index (HDI)	0.761 (85th out of 189 countries)
Individuals using the Internet	70.4% of total population (2020)
Renewable energy consumption	14.5% of total energy consumption (2019)

Shanghai

> **Key Point**
>
> China is the world's largest importer and exporter of goods.

Gobi Desert

Alpine tundra

> **Key Words**
>
> sub-tropical
> tropical rainforest
> cold desert
> alpine tundra
> One Child Policy
> catchment area
> earthquake
> Richter scale
> manufacturing
> Communist

Quick Test

1. Name three crops grown in China.
2. How many births did the One Child Policy prevent between 1979 and 2015 and what is the current limit on children per couple?
3. Name the longest river in China and give its length.
4. Which political party is in power in China?

Location Knowledge – India

Quick Recall Quiz

You must be able to:

- Describe the environmental regions of India
- Understand the key physical and human characteristics of India
- Name the major cities of India.

Environmental Regions

- The Himalayas have an **alpine tundra** climate where snow lies on the ground all year round.
- The Indo-Gangetic Plain in the north of India has a **humid sub-tropical** climate with hot, wet summers and cold, dry winters. It is 700 000 km^2 and was formed from the sediments of the rivers that flow from the Himalayas. Thick forests grow here and the region is farmed for rice, wheat, maize, sugar cane and cotton.
- The Thar Desert is a **hot desert** found in north-west India. It is over 200 000 km^2 and temperatures range from 5°C in the winter to 50°C in the summer.
- The Deccan Plateau rises approximately 600 m above sea level and covers 1.3 million km^2 of central and southern India. It is a **semi-arid** region with vegetation that varies from thorn bushes to forests and wildlife including tigers and Indian elephants. Tea and coffee plantations are found on the Deccan Plateau.
- The Western Ghats mountain range, on the west coast of southern India, has a **tropical wet** climate where temperatures do not fall below 18°C and tropical forests grow.

The Himalayas

Physical and Human Characteristics

- India is the seventh largest country in the world covering 3 287 263 km^2.
- India has a **monsoon** climate with four seasons:
   Winter: December to March.
  2 Summer (dry season): April to June.
  3 Monsoon (rainy season): July to September.
  4 Autumn: October to November.
- India has three major rivers: the Indus (3180 km), which flows through Pakistan, Tibet and India; the Ganges (2525 km), which flows through India and Bangladesh; and the Brahmaputra (2900 km), which flows through Tibet, India and Bangladesh.
- India's economy has grown at an annual rate of about 5% in the 21st century. Major Indian industries include motor vehicles, shipbuilding, chemicals, telecommunications, computers, software development, pharmaceuticals, textiles, agriculture and mining.

Key Point

Over 80% of people in India are Hindus, 13% are Muslim, 2% are Christian and the remaining 5% are mainly Sikh or Buddhist.

Key Point

Despite significant increases in wages since 2000, 21% of India's population still live on less than $2 a day.

- The population of India is 1.4 billion (2022 estimate), making it the second most populous country in the world after China.
- There are nearly 50 cities in India with a population of 1 million or more. Delhi, the area that includes the capital New Delhi, is the most populous (32 million, according to a 2022 estimate), followed by Mumbai (21 million in 2022) and Bangalore (13 million in 2022).
- India used to be part of the **British Empire** but gained its **independence** in 1947 under the leadership of Jawaharlal Nehru. India is now the world's largest **democracy** with six main political parties and general elections held every five years.

Development Indicators for India	
Gross Domestic Product (GDP) (per capita)	$2543
Employment structure	Primary 43%; Secondary 25%; Tertiary & Quaternary 32%
Birth rate (per 1000) Death rate (per 1000) Natural increase (per 1000)	17.1 7.3 9.8
Life expectancy	70.2 years
Literacy rate	Male: 82.4%; Female 65.8% (2019)
Human Development Index (HDI)	0.647 (131st out of 189 countries)
Individuals using the Internet	43% of total population (2020)
Renewable energy consumption	32.9% of total energy consumption (2019)

Mumbai

Western Ghats

Thar Desert

Key Words

alpine tundra
humid sub-tropical
hot desert
semi-arid
tropical wet
monsoon
British Empire
independence
democracy

Quick Test

1. Name the type of environment found in the Himalayas.
2. When does India's rainy season (monsoon) take place?
3. Which is the longest river that flows through India?
4. When did India gain its independence from the British Empire?

Location Knowledge – The Middle East

You must be able to:

- Describe the environmental regions of the Middle East
- Understand the key physical and human characteristics of the Middle East
- Name the major cities of the Middle East.

Environmental Regions

- Most of the Middle East is hot desert. This includes the Egyptian section of the Sahara Desert and the Arabian Desert, which covers 2.3 million km^2 of the Arabian Peninsula.
- The Arabian Desert includes the Rub' al-Khali or 'Empty Quarter' which, at 650 000 km^2, is the largest sand desert in the world, with 250 m high sand dunes. Rainfall here is less than 30 mm a year.
- Western Turkey has a **Mediterranean climate** characterised by warm, wet winters and hot, dry summers. Typical Mediterranean vegetation includes pine, cedar, olive and citrus trees, and shrubs and bushes such as lavender and rosemary.

Physical and Human Characteristics

- The Middle East is an area of mainly West Asian countries located between Africa, Europe and Central Asia.
- The Middle East covers an area of 6.5 million km^2 and has a population of approximately 438 million. High population densities are found near sources of water (rivers and lakes).
- A number of narrow waterways carry trade into and out of the Middle East, including the Suez Canal, linking the Mediterranean Sea to the Red Sea; Bab el-Mandeb, a strait that separates the Red Sea from the Indian Ocean; and the Strait of Hormuz, linking the Gulf and the Indian Ocean.
- About 50 ships per day pass through the Suez Canal (about 12% of total global trade) but in 2021 it was blocked for six days by a 400-metre long vessel that became wedged across the waterway.
- The three largest rivers in the Middle East are the Nile in Egypt (6650 km), the Euphrates that flows through Turkey, Syria and Iraq (2800 km) and the Tigris, which flows through Turkey and joins the Euphrates in Iraq (1850 km).
- 60% of the population are **Arabs**, an **ethnic group** from the Arabian Peninsula, who speak **Arabic**. Other significant ethnic groups in the Middle East are Persians, Turks, Kurds and Jews (the latter make up 85% of the population of Israel).
- **Islam** is the main religion in most Middle Eastern countries and most **Muslims** follow the Sunni sect of Islam. There are significant numbers of Christians in Lebanon, Egypt and Israel.

> **Key Point**
>
> The countries of the Middle East are: Bahrain, Cyprus, Egypt, Iran, Iraq, Israel, Jordan, Kuwait, Lebanon, Oman, Qatar, Saudi Arabia, Syria, Turkey, United Arab Emirates and Yemen. Gaza and West Bank are disputed territories.

Arabian Desert, UAE

Suez Canal

- The total annual **Gross Domestic Product (GDP)** in the Middle East was $3.6 trillion in 2021. But the GDP of individual countries ranged from $690 per capita in Yemen to $61 276 per capita in Qatar.
- The largest cities in the Middle East are:
  - Cairo in Egypt (21.75 million)
  - Istanbul in Turkey (15.6 million)
  - Tehran in Iran (9 million)
  - Riyadh in Saudi Arabia (7.6 million)
  - Baghdad in Iraq (7.2 million).

Development Indicators for the Middle East	
Gross Domestic Product (GDP) (per capita)	$17 621 (average)
Birth rate (per 1000) Death rate (per 1000) Natural increase (per 1000)	18.5 4.1 14.4
Life expectancy	Yemen (lowest): 66 years – Israel (highest): 82.6 years
Literacy rate	Male: 85.1%; Female 72.4% (2019)
Human Development Index (HDI)	Israel 0.919 (19th out of 189 countries) – Yemen 0.470 (179th out of 189 countries)
Individuals using the Internet	73.6% of total population (2020)
Renewable energy consumption	5.6% of total energy consumption (2019)

Dubai, in the UAE

Quick Test

1. How large is the Arabian Desert?
2. What is special about the Rub' al-Khali?
3. Which is the largest ethnic group in the Middle East?
4. Name two religions practised in the Middle East.

Revise

Key Point

The richest countries of the Middle East gain their wealth from exporting oil. These countries include Qatar, Bahrain, the United Arab Emirates, Kuwait, Saudi Arabia, Oman, Iraq and Iran.

Cairo

Key Words

Mediterranean climate
Arab
ethnic group
Arabic
Islam
Muslim
Gross Domestic Product (GDP)

Africa and Asia Compared – Kenya

Quick Recall Quiz

You must be able to:

- Describe and explain the physical and human geography of Kenya
- Understand the similarities and differences between Kenya and other places
- Understand the links between Kenya and other places.

Physical Characteristics

- Kenya covers an area of 582 650 km², more than twice the area of the UK.
- Kenya is on the **Equator** giving it a tropical climate where the Sun stays overhead all year.
- Kenya has two rainy seasons: the 'long rains' from April to June and the 'short rains' from October to December. Total annual rainfall for Kenya is 1390 mm (similar to the UK's).
- The hot dry season is from January to March (average temperature 29°C) and the cool dry season is from July to September (average temperature 26°C).
- Being on the Equator also means that the times of sunrise and sunset stay the same all year (6:00–6:30 am and 6:30–7:00 pm).
- Kenya has five main environmental zones:
  1. Steppe, consisting of desert-like scrub and grassland, covering most of the north and east.
  2. Hot desert in the far north.
  3. **Tropical equatorial forest** on the east coast.
  4. **Savannah grasslands** covering the south.
  5. **Montane forest** in the Kenyan Highlands of Western Kenya (tropical evergreen forests with high temperatures and humidity, and high densities of orchids, ferns, mosses and lichen).
- Kenya's highest mountain is Mt Kenya at 5119 m. It is a stratovolcano, formed over three million years ago.
- The Great Rift Valley runs through the west of Kenya. It is being formed as the African tectonic plate splits in two and has been partially filled by lakes such as Lake Turkana.

> **Key Point**
>
> The savannah is the most well-known environmental region in Kenya. It consists of vast plains of grass with scattered trees such as the baobab and acacia. The savannah is where the majority of Kenya's wildlife is to be found, such as giraffe, lion, elephant, leopard, cheetah, hippo and rhinoceros.

Human Characteristics

- The population of Kenya was 56.1 million in 2020.
- Kenya has a very young population, with an average age of 19.7. 60% of the population is under the age of 25 and only 8% is over the age of 55. (In the UK, 23% of people are aged over 60.)
- Annual population growth in Kenya is 2.2%, which means an extra million people in Kenya each year.
- Kenya is a poor country, sometimes defined as less economically developed. It struggles to cope with rapid population growth.

On safari

- The Maasai are a distinctive ethnic group in Kenya who are **nomadic pastoralists**. In 2019 there were approximately 1.2 million Maasai in Kenya. The Maasai move their herds of cattle around the Kenyan savannah and steppe in search of water and grazing.
- The largest city in Kenya, and the capital, is Nairobi, with a population of 5.2 million. Kenya's second largest city is Mombasa, population 1.4 million.
- Kenya was a **colony** of the British Empire from 1888 to 1963 when it gained independence under the leadership of President Jomo Kenyatta.
- Brooke Bond has been growing and selling tea in Kenya since the 1920s. It is now owned by Unilever and produces 32 million kilograms of tea a year.
- Kenya exports 35 000 tonnes of flowers to Europe each year. Kenyan flowers are sold by the main British supermarkets.
- In 2019, 2.5 million tourists visited Kenya (180 000 of these were from the UK). Most tourists come to Kenya to go on safari to view the wildlife in the national parks and to enjoy the coral reefs and tropical beaches on the east coast near Mombasa.
- Tourism accounts for 25% of Kenya's export earnings (money that comes in to Kenya from other countries) and tourism employs 800 000 people.

Maasai

Kenyan beach

Key Point

Kenya's main exports are tea (18%), flowers (12%) and coffee (5%), which are grown in the Kenyan Highlands.

Development Indicators for Kenya	
Gross Domestic Product (GDP) (per capita)	$2007
Employment structure	Primary 54%; Secondary & Tertiary 46%
Birth rate (per 1000) Death rate (per 1000) Natural increase (per 1000)	28 5 23
Life expectancy	67 years
Literacy rate	Male 85%; Female 78.2% (2019)
Human Development Index (HDI)	0.601 (143rd out of 189 countries)
Individuals using the Internet	29.5% of total population (2020)
Renewable energy consumption	68.1% of total energy consumption (2019)

Key Words

Equator
tropical equatorial forest
savannah grasslands
montane forest
nomadic pastoralists
colony

Quick Test

1. How large is Kenya?
2. When does Kenya experience its highest temperatures?
3. What is the capital of Kenya?

Quick Recall Quiz

Africa and Asia Compared – South Korea

You must be able to:

- Describe and explain the physical and human geography of South Korea
- Understand the similarities and differences between South Korea and other places
- Understand the links between South Korea and other places.

Physical Characteristics

- South Korea is in East Asia and is part of the Korean Peninsula extending south from China into the Pacific Ocean.
- The area of South Korea is 99 617 km^2, less than half the size of the UK.
- Most of South Korea is mountainous; only 30% of the land area is suitable for building and agriculture.
- South Korea's highest mountain is Hallasan, a 1950 m high extinct volcano on the island of Jeju in the Korea Strait between South Korea and Japan.
- South Korea has a temperate monsoon climate. Annual temperatures range from –7°C to 29°C. Average annual rainfall varies between 600 mm in the north and 1500 mm in the south.
- The longest rivers in South Korea are the Nakdong (521 km) and the Han (510 km).
- Most of South Korea's forests have been cut down but there is some tropical forest on the south coast. Patches of deciduous and coniferous forest can be found throughout South Korea containing oak, birch, spruce and yew trees.
- South Korea is affected by **tropical typhoons**. In 2012, Typhoon Bolaven struck with 186 km/h (116 mph) winds. 19 people were killed in South Korea and at least 50 more in North Korea. 1.9 million homes lost power and damage costing $374.3 million was caused.

South Korea

Volcanic crater at the summit of Mount Hallasan

Human Characteristics

- The population of South Korea was 51.3 million in 2022.
- The capital of South Korea is Seoul, its largest city, with a population of 9.9 million (2022).
- South Korea is a developed country with the tenth largest economy in the world and it is the world's fifth largest exporter.
- It is home to global electronics and vehicle manufacturers including Samsung, LG, Daewoo, Hyundai and Kia (these large companies are known as **chaebols**).
- In 1945, Korea was liberated from Japan, which had ruled the country as a colonial power, by Soviet forces in the north and American forces in the south. The country was divided in two.

Traditional house

- In 1950, a civil war began when North Korea invaded South Korea. A ceasefire was declared in 1953 after three million deaths; the contested border between the two had barely moved at all.
- In 1953, South Korea was an extremely poor country with a gross domestic product (GDP) per capita of $872 (in the UK the GDP per capita in 1953 was $11 972; in Kenya it was $339).
- In 1953, General Park Chung Hee took over the government and made changes that brought about rapid economic growth:
  - New roads were built to open up the country.
  - The government took over control of factories.
  - The government concentrated on the manufacturing industry including shipbuilding, vehicle manufacture, textiles and electronics.
  - New schools were built.
- In 1987, the first free elections were held. By then, 99% of people owned a television and most had fridges and washing machines.
- South Korea now has free trade agreements with the UK and the European Union, which encourages greater trade owing to the removal of tariffs on many imported and exported goods.

Development Indicators for South Korea	
Gross Domestic Product (GDP) (per capita)	$31 489
Employment structure	Primary 5%; Secondary 24%; Tertiary & Quaternary 71%
Birth rate (per 1000) Death rate (per 1000) Natural increase (per 1000)	6.9 6.6 0.3
Life expectancy	83.3 years
Literacy rate	Male: 99.2%; Female 96.6% (2019)
Human Development Index (HDI)	0.916 (23rd out of 189 countries)
Individuals using the Internet	96.5% of total population (2020)
Renewable energy consumption	3.4% of total energy consumption (2019)

Key Point

Between 1953 and 1987 South Korea's economy grew rapidly to a GDP per capita of $7455 whereas Kenya's GDP per capita had grown to only $583.

Seoul

Quick Test

1. How much of South Korea is lowland?
2. What type of climate does South Korea have?
3. What was the population of South Korea in 2022?

Key Words

tropical typhoon
chaebol

Geological Timescale 1

You must be able to:

- Explain what the Geological Timescale is and how it is constructed
- Explain what fossils are and why they are important
- Understand how living things have evolved over time.

The Geological Timescale

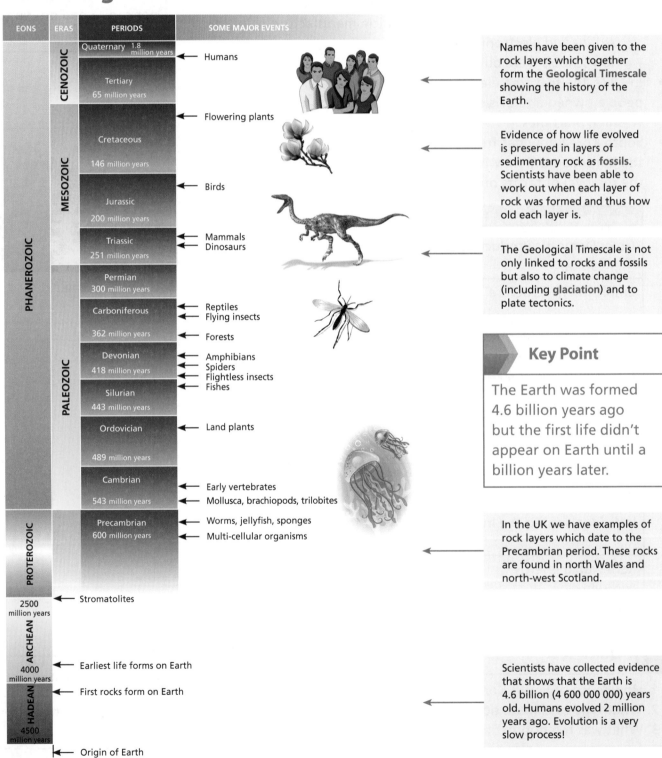

EONS	ERAS	PERIODS	SOME MAJOR EVENTS
PHANEROZOIC	CENOZOIC	Quaternary 1.8 million years	Humans
		Tertiary 65 million years	
	MESOZOIC	Cretaceous 146 million years	Flowering plants
		Jurassic 200 million years	Birds
		Triassic 251 million years	Mammals / Dinosaurs
	PALEOZOIC	Permian 300 million years	
		Carboniferous 362 million years	Reptiles / Flying insects / Forests
		Devonian 418 million years	Amphibians / Spiders / Flightless insects / Fishes
		Silurian 443 million years	
		Ordovician 489 million years	Land plants
		Cambrian 543 million years	Early vertebrates / Mollusca, brachiopods, trilobites
PROTEROZOIC		Precambrian 600 million years	Worms, jellyfish, sponges / Multi-cellular organisms
		2500 million years	Stromatolites
ARCHEAN		4000 million years	Earliest life forms on Earth
HADEAN		4500 million years	First rocks form on Earth
			Origin of Earth

Names have been given to the rock layers which together form the **Geological Timescale** showing the history of the Earth.

Evidence of how life evolved is preserved in layers of sedimentary rock as **fossils**. Scientists have been able to work out when each layer of rock was formed and thus how old each layer is.

The Geological Timescale is not only linked to rocks and fossils but also to climate change (including **glaciation**) and to plate tectonics.

Key Point

The Earth was formed 4.6 billion years ago but the first life didn't appear on Earth until a billion years later.

In the UK we have examples of rock layers which date to the Precambrian period. These rocks are found in north Wales and north-west Scotland.

Scientists have collected evidence that shows that the Earth is 4.6 billion (4 600 000 000) years old. Humans evolved 2 million years ago. Evolution is a very slow process!

The Fossil Record

- Present-day plants and animals are different to those that have been preserved as fossils. It wasn't until Charles Darwin wrote a book in the 19th century describing his theory of **evolution** that the fossil record was properly understood.
- Darwin said that, over time, living things change and develop new characteristics. Those creatures that are best adapted to their environment survive and those that are not, become **extinct**.
- When the Earth was first formed, there was no life. The first simple life forms appeared after about 1 billion years; these life forms were microscopic and lived in the sea. Eventually, around 450 million years ago, the first plants and animals colonised the land. Reptiles and flying insects appeared around 350 million years ago.
- The dinosaurs were the dominant life forms on Earth for around 160 million years. Scientists believe they became extinct after an asteroid struck the Earth. Modern-day birds evolved from the dinosaurs.
- Humans have only lived on Earth for a very short period of time. If the entire Geological Timescale was reduced to a single day, humans would have been around for about a minute:

  1. The Earth is formed at midnight.
  2. At 4.00 am the first simple life appears.
  3. At 10.46 pm the dinosaurs appear.
  4. At 11.58 pm and 43 seconds, the first humans appear!

- Humans are primates and descended from apes. Humans belong to a group of apes called 'hominids'.
- The first humans appeared around 2.3 million years ago in Africa. These early humans learnt to use fire and simple tools. They survived by hunting and gathering wild food.
- Modern-day humans are called Homo sapiens and have much larger brains than their early ancestors.
- Scientists have studied the evolution of humans from the remains of skeletons, particularly skulls, preserved in the soil. Using modern technology, they can work out what humans looked like in the past.

A fossilised fish

A Tyrannosaurus-Rex skeleton

Key Point

Life on Earth evolves very slowly and humans have only appeared on Earth in very recent times.

Quick Test

1. How old is the Earth?
2. Who first wrote about the theory of evolution?
3. Where would you find the oldest rocks in the UK?
4. For how long did dinosaurs live on Earth?

Key Words

Geological Timescale
fossil
glaciation
evolution
extinct

Geological Timescale 2

Quick Recall Quiz

You must be able to:

- Understand that the climate of the Earth has changed over millions of years
- Describe the effects of these climate changes
- Understand how the continents have changed position due to plate tectonics.

Changing Climates

- The climate of the Earth has changed many times in the past. Indeed when the Earth was first formed, it had no atmosphere. The young Earth would have been very hot with no water.
- Several times in the Earth's history the planet has become cooler. This has resulted in ice spreading from the polar regions across the land and oceans. These are called **ice ages** and the process of glaciation has helped to shape the surface of the Earth.
- The most recent ice age only finished about 11 700 years ago. Much of the UK was covered in an ice sheet at this point.
- During an ice age, the climate alternates between extreme cold for thousands of years (a **glacial period**) and then much warmer conditions (an **interglacial period**).
- In the last 100 years, humans have released a great deal of air pollution from factories and transport. These greenhouse gases trap heat in the atmosphere and cause the average temperature of the Earth to increase. This is contributing to **global warming**. Human activity that produces greenhouse gases is called the **enhanced greenhouse effect**.
- Glaciation is important because it affects **sea level**. When a lot of water is trapped on the land as ice, the sea level falls. When the ice melts, the sea level rises again.
- Most climate scientists agree that human activity is accelerating global warming and, therefore, further rises in sea level.
- If all the ice at the polar regions melted, sea level would be much higher than at present and large areas would be flooded. This has happened many times in the geologic past.
- About 100 million years ago, during the Cretaceous period, much of the UK was under a warm tropical sea and the remains of small marine animals settled on the sea floor to form chalk.
- Over time, the rocks have been squeezed upwards and sea level has fallen. The chalk and the fossils formed in it can now be seen in the hills and cliffs of south-east England.

> **Key Point**
>
> The global climate has changed many times in the past. During glacial periods it has been much colder.

> **Key Point**
>
> During the last glaciation, early humans moved south to escape the cold weather and animals such as the woolly mammoth became specially adapted to living in freezing conditions.

An alpine glacier

Air pollution from industry

Moving Plates

- The Earth's crust is divided into many different sections called tectonic plates. These plates move a few centimetres per year. Although this seems very little, over millions of years it means the plates move hundreds, even thousands, of kilometres.
- The same fossils are found in Africa and South America. How is this possible? The answer is that millions of years ago, these two continents were joined together but have since slowly moved apart. This is called **continental drift**.
- Cynognathus was a large Triassic reptile, three metres long. Its remains have been found in both central Africa and central South America in sedimentary rocks that were formed around 250 million years ago. This happened when all the land masses formed a single continent called Pangaea (see page 22).
- During the Permian period, around 300 million years ago, the UK was located much further south. Being closer to the Equator, it had a desert climate. Evidence of this is found in red sandstone rocks that cover a large part of central England (Cheshire, Shropshire and Yorkshire).

200 million years ago

Today

(see page 22)

Key Point

The plates that form the Earth's crust move around very slowly and the continents that we know today were not always in the positions they are now.

Quick Test

1. What was the atmosphere of the Earth like when the Earth was first formed?
2. Why was the woolly mammoth woolly?
3. Where does air pollution come from?
4. How fast do the Earth's plates move?

Key Words

ice age
glacial period
interglacial period
global warming
sea level

Plate Tectonics 1

You must be able to:

- Understand the structure of the Earth
- Describe the different plate boundaries
- Understand the effects of plate movements.

Structure of the Earth

- The Earth is a rocky planet that formed billions of years ago.
- At the centre of the Earth is a hot but solid metal **core**. Scientists have calculated that the temperature is 5000°C. The core gives out heat that passes through the Earth.
- Around the core is a thick layer of semi-molten rock called the **mantle**. The hot rocks in the mantle are able to slowly flow.
- Around the outside of the Earth is a thin, solid layer called the **crust**. The crust is broken into a large number of separate sections called **tectonic plates**:
  - The plates that form the oceanic crust are relatively thin (up to 6 km), with oceans such as the Atlantic lying on top.
  - The plates that form the continental crust are much thicker (5–70 km) and form the main land masses such as Europe.
- Where two plates meet is called a **plate boundary**.
- The plates are constantly moving and changing position; for example, the plate that carries the UK was once much further south and the UK then had a desert climate.
- Many millions of years ago, all the continents were joined together in a single super-continent known as Pangaea. This super-continent split up into different sections as the crustal plates moved and this created the modern-day continents.
- Movement is still happening and each year the UK, on the Eurasian Plate, gets further away from the USA, which lies on the North American Plate.

Plate Boundaries

- There are three types of plate boundary and the movement of the plates is different at each one.
- Movement along the plate boundaries causes earthquakes and volcanoes.

Structure of the Earth

Crust – up to 70 km thick

Core – has liquid outer part and solid inner part (3500 km thick)

Mantle – has properties of a solid but flows very slowly (2800 km thick)

Key Point

The Earth's crust is broken into sections called plates. These plates move very slowly in different directions.

Tectonic plates

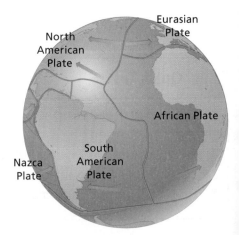

Eurasian Plate

North American Plate

African Plate

Nazca Plate

South American Plate

At a **destructive plate boundary**, the plates are moving towards each other. The plates get squeezed together and one plate (oceanic) slides under the other (continental). This is called **subduction**. The subducted plate melts and forms magma.

The squeezing of the rocks due to great heat and pressure causes the land to rise and mountains to form. The Himalayas in Asia are still rising due to these powerful forces.

There are often volcanoes at destructive plate margins and the plates rubbing against each other can also cause earthquakes.

At a **constructive plate boundary**, the plates are moving away from each other. Molten magma rises up through the gaps created by this process, cools, hardens and forms new land.

Most constructive plate boundaries occur under the oceans and this creates underwater volcanoes which may form volcanic islands such as Iceland.

In East Africa, the Great Rift Valley is one of the few examples of a constructive plate boundary on land. This part of Africa is splitting in two. Where Arabia has split from the rest of Africa, water has filled the crack to form the Red Sea.

At a **conservative plate boundary**, land is neither being created nor destroyed as two plates are simply sliding past each other. The main consequence of this is earthquakes, some of which may have disastrous results.

The most famous conservative plate boundary is the San Andreas Fault in California, USA. In 1906, a devastating earthquake flattened San Francisco destroying over half the homes and killing around 3000 people.

Quick Test

1. Which layer in the Earth is hottest?
2. What are the sections of the crust called?
3. The Himalayas have been formed at which type of plate boundary?
4. The San Andreas Fault is an example of which type of plate boundary?

Key Words

core
mantle
crust
tectonic plate
plate boundary
destructive boundary
constructive boundary
conservative boundary

Plate Tectonics 2

You must be able to:

- Understand what an earthquake is and why they happen
- Understand what a volcano is and why they erupt
- Describe the dangers caused by these two natural disasters.

Earthquakes

- An **earthquake** is a violent shaking of part of the Earth's crust. Thousands of tiny earthquakes happen every day. For example, in Japan they can have 1000 tremors a day, which can result in two or three earthquakes each day!
- Earthquakes are caused by a sudden movement of the rocks along a plate boundary. The most damaging earthquakes happen along destructive and conservative plate boundaries.
- This sudden movement sends out shockwaves, which quickly travel through the rocks of the crust:
  - The point at which the shockwaves start, usually deep underground is called the **focus** of the earthquake.
  - The point at which the shockwaves reach the surface and cause damage is called the **epicentre**.
- Shockwaves slowly lose their power as they move through the rocks so the most damage is done at the epicentre and damage decreases as you move away from this point.
- If an earthquake occurs under the ocean, the movement of the seabed may cause a powerful wave called a **tsunami**.
- In 2004 a tsunami in the Indian Ocean killed almost a quarter of a million people and affected 14 different countries. With waves up to 30 m (100 ft) high, it was one of the deadliest natural disasters in recorded history.

The Aftermath of Earthquakes

- As the ground shakes during an earthquake, it may crack. This causes damage to buildings, roads, railways and bridges. Underground pipes and cables can be broken leading to gas escaping and fires breaking out.
- After an earthquake, thousands of people may be left homeless without easy access to shelter, food or clean water. As a result, many people may die in the weeks after the earthquake.
- Vital buildings such as hospitals, schools and police stations may also be destroyed.
- International aid may be sent from other countries to help the victims of the earthquake. This can include tents, bottled water and food.
- Experts with special equipment and sniffer dogs may also be sent to help search for people trapped in the wreckage.

> **Key Point**
>
> Earthquakes can cause death and destruction but fortunately these are rare. Earthquakes are most common along the edges of the plates.

Earthquake features

City
Earthquake epicentre
Shockwaves
Earthquake focus
Fault line
Crust

Buildings destroyed

Damaged infrastructure

Volcanoes

- A **volcano** is a mountain formed from molten rock ejected from a hole in the Earth's crust. Pressure in the molten rock can build up over hundreds of years.
- Volcanoes occur on land and under the sea.
- Volcanoes are formed along the edges of constructive and destructive plate boundaries. A line of volcanoes is found along the west coast of the USA where the Pacific Plate meets the North American Plate, for example.
- A few volcanoes are also created in other areas called **hot spots**. These are weaknesses in the Earth's crust where molten magma can escape to the surface and cool as lava. The Hawaiian islands are examples of hot spot volcanoes.
- A volcano will consist of either lava on its own or alternating layers of lava and ash.
- If the lava is very runny, the volcano will be very wide but not very tall. These are shield volcanoes. The volcanoes in Hawaii are this shape.
- If the lava is thick and sticky, it can form tall, narrow volcanoes. These are composite volcanoes. Mount St Helens (USA), Mount Fuji (Japan) and Mount Etna (Italy) are this shape.

Runny lava in Hawaii

- People like to live near volcanoes because the land can be fertile and good for growing crops.
- Despite the dangers, many people still live near volcanoes because predicting when they will erupt is very accurate. If scientists think a volcano is going to erupt, people may have to be evacuated to a safe place. Hot lava or ash can damage buildings and kill or injure people.
- Eventually, most volcanoes become **dormant** and stop erupting.

> **Key Point**
>
> Volcanoes can bring benefits to humans but they are also dangerous when they erupt.

> **Key Words**
>
> earthquake
> focus
> epicentre
> tsunami
> volcano
> dormant

Quick Test

1. How common are tiny earthquakes?
2. What is the focus of an earthquake?
3. Why are fires common after an earthquake?
4. What is lava?

Practice Questions

Location Knowledge – Russia, China, India and the Middle East

1   **a)** Why does the majority of Russia's agriculture take place in the steppe regions?   [2]

     b) Underline the correct words in the following sentences.

        In Russia's semi-arid regions, temperatures can reach **38°C / 58°C / 80°C**.
Rainfall is less than **250 mm / 500 mm / 750 mm** per year.   [2]

2   **a) i)** What is the capital city of Russia?   [1]

        ii) What is its population?   [1]

     b) Suggest two reasons why Russia's population is stagnating.   [4]

3   Why do you think China's economy has grown so quickly in the last 30 years?
Tick (✓) the correct answers.

People can own and run their own businesses.   ☐

People are spending less.   ☐

The government has encouraged international trade.   ☐

People don't like to work hard.   ☐   [2]

4   Why is the Indo-Gangetic plain in India so good for agriculture?   [3]

5   **a)** Give reasons for India's rapid population growth.   [3]

     b) Why are so many people in India living on $1.25 a day when it has the fifth largest economy in the world?   [2]

6   Why was Jawaharlal Nehru important in India's history?   [4]

7   **a)** How much land area does the Middle East cover?   [1]

     b) Which three continents have countries that are part of the Middle East?
Tick (✓) the correct options.

Europe	☐	North America	☐
South America	☐	Africa	☐
Asia	☐	Australasia	☐

[3]

8   Why is the Suez Canal such an important waterway?   [3]

Africa and Asia Compared – Kenya and South Korea

1 **a)** Where is the Rift Valley in Kenya? [1]

b) How was the Rift Valley formed? [3]

2 Which of the following are Kenya's three main exports?
Tick (✓) the correct answers.

Rice ☐   Coffee ☐

Tea ☐   Cocoa ☐

Cotton ☐   Flowers ☐ [3]

3 Why is the rate of population growth in Kenya a problem for the country? [3]

4 **a)** Fill in the gaps in the following sentences:

In 2019, _____ tourists visited Kenya. They come to Kenya mainly

to go on _____ and to visit the beaches near Kenya's second

largest city, _____. [3]

b) Why is tourism so important to Kenya? [3]

5 What is meant by the term 'chaebol'? [2]

6 **a)** List the methods used by the South Korean government to achieve rapid economic growth. [4]

b) How did South Korea's GDP change between 1953 and 1987? [2]

7 Tick (✓) the boxes next to the statements which are true.

South Korea's longest river is the Nakdong River. ☐

South Korea's capital city is Nairobi. ☐

A free trade agreement exists between the EU and South Korea. ☐ [2]

8 **a)** When did Typhoon Bolaven hit South Korea? [1]

b) What impact did the typhoon have on the country? [3]

Practice Questions

Geological Timescale

1 **a)** What is the Geological Timescale? [2]

    b) How long after the Earth was formed did the first life forms appear? [1]

    c) What is a fossil? [2]

2 Which group of animals did birds evolve from?

    Tick (✓) the correct option.

    Reptiles ☐

    Dinosaurs ☐

    Early vertebrates ☐

    Molluscs ☐ [1]

3 What are hominids? [1]

4 Why did it not rain when the Earth was first formed? [1]

5 **a)** How did humans survive the very cold weather during the last glaciation? [2]

    b) During a glaciation, what happens to sea level and why? [2]

6 What effect do greenhouse gases have on the Earth's climate?

    Tick (✓) the correct options.

    Greenhouse gases allow heat out of the atmosphere. ☐

    Greenhouse gases trap heat in the atmosphere. ☐

    The climate becomes warmer. ☐

    The climate becomes cooler. ☐ [2]

Plate Tectonics

1 **a)** Label the diagram of the Earth.

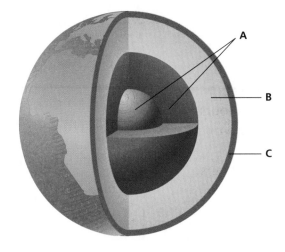

[3]

b) Why might the Earth's crust be described as being as thin as an eggshell? [1]

c) What is the estimated temperature of the Earth's core? [1]

d) What effect does the heat from the core have on the mantle layer? [2]

2 What name is given to the ancient super-continent before it broke up into the modern-day continents? [1]

3 **a)** What is an earthquake? [1]

b) What happens at the epicentre of an earthquake and why? [2]

4 Why did the 2004 Indian Ocean tsunami kill so many people? [2]

5 What is international aid? Give an example. [2]

6 Tick (✓) the statements that are true.

All volcanoes are made of lava and ash. ☐

Volcanoes in Hawaii are low and wide. ☐

A dormant volcano is one which has recently erupted. ☐

Land near volcanoes is fertile. ☐ [2]

Rocks and Geology 1

Quick Recall Quiz

You must be able to:

- Understand the difference between porous and non-porous rocks
- Identify the three types of rock: sedimentary, igneous and metamorphic
- Understand how the different types of rock form.

What are Rocks?

- All rocks are made up of grains and every grain is a **mineral**.
- The grains in the rock can be different shapes, sizes and colours, and how they fit together decides whether it will be a hard or soft rock.
- **Porous** rocks with round grains have spaces or gaps. Water gets into them and the rock is often soft and crumbly.
- **Non-porous** rocks have tightly fitting grains and water cannot get in.

Types of Rock

- **Sedimentary** rocks are formed from deposits originally eroded from older rocks and living organisms:
  1. Rocks (igneous, metamorphic or other sedimentary rocks) are weakened by weathering and worn away by erosion.
  2. Worn away material is transported as fragments or dissolved in water and carried by ice, gravity, wind, sea and rivers.
  3. Transported material is eventually deposited (laid down) in shallow seas, lakes or hollows in the landscape. These deposits form beds of sediment (layers).
  4. Some beds might be the remains of living things. For example, coal beds are formed from the remains of ancient plants.
  5. Beds of sediment are compacted (pressed and squeezed together) as the weight of sediment increases. In the end all the loose sediment is stratified (layered) and cemented (joined) into solid rock (**lithified**).
  6. Remember: there are pores (spaces) between the sediments. This weakens the rock, so sedimentary rocks are said to be soft.
- This process can take millions of years. New sedimentary rock is being formed all the time on the ocean bed.
- Examples include chalk, limestone, sandstone, shale, clay, coal, conglomerate and breccia.

Carboniferous sandstone
The sandy grains in this rock leave spaces between one another. It is soft, crumbly and porous. This specimen formed during the Carboniferous period 299 to 358 million years ago and shows a fossilised fish.

Key Point

To name a rock and understand how it is formed, a geologist asks: 'What minerals does it contain, and how are the minerals held together?'

Key Point

Sedimentary rock makes up 7% of the Earth's crust.

Eroded sedimentary rock can create dramatic features

Key Point

Igneous rock makes up 65% of the Earth's crust.

- **Igneous** rocks are formed when magma cools and solidifies:
  1. The inside of the Earth is very hot – hot enough to melt rocks. Molten rock is called magma.
  2. Magma tends to rise upwards in the Earth's crust. If it spills out on to the surface it is called lava.
  3. As magma cools it forms igneous rocks.
  4. As magma cools its mineral crystals begin to grow.
  5. The slower the magma cools the bigger the crystals.
  6. Igneous rocks are hard and **crystalline**. There are no obvious pores in igneous rocks.
- Examples include granite, gabbro, basalt, pumice, obsidian and volcanic ash.

Granite
The grains fit tightly together in this rock so it is hard and non-porous. This rock formed between 354 and 417 million years ago.

- **Metamorphic** rocks are formed when heat and/or pressure cause rocks to change without melting.
  1. Movements in the Earth can cause rocks to be deeply buried, squashing them or moving them closer to molten magma.
  2. Heat and pressure cause the chemical elements in the original rock to react and re-form into new minerals.
  3. As metamorphism occurs, no elements are taken and none added; they are simply rearranged.
  4. Remember that metamorphic rocks do not form from melted rock – melting causes igneous rocks to form.
  5. The new minerals in metamorphic rocks have crystals that are arranged in layers.
  6. Metamorphic rocks can be formed from sedimentary or igneous rocks.
- Examples include marble, slate, schist and gneiss.

> ### Quick Test
>
> 1. Which type of rock tends to be softer – porous or non-porous?
> 2. Rearrange these terms into the correct order so they show the processes by which sedimentary rocks form:
>   lithification / transportation / erosion / deposition
> 3. What is molten rock called?
> 4. Which type of rock forms from molten rock?

> ## Revise

> ### Key Point
>
> **Extrusive** igneous rocks have cooled quickly outside the Earth. **Intrusive** igneous rocks have cooled slowly inside the Earth.

Rock types in Earth's crust

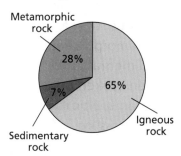

Metamorphic rock 28%
Igneous rock 65%
Sedimentary rock 7%

> ### Key Point
>
> Metamorphic rock makes up 28% of the Earth's crust.

A piece of metamorphic rock that has been changed by heat and pressure

> ### Key Words
>
> **mineral**
> **porous**
> **non-porous**
> **sedimentary**
> **lithified**
> **igneous**
> **crystalline**
> **extrusive**
> **intrusive**
> **metamorphic**

Rocks and Geology 2

You must be able to:

- Explain the rock cycle
- Understand how weathering and erosion affect rocks.

Quick Recall Quiz

The Rock Cycle

- The rocks that make up the Earth are recycled and do not stay the same forever.
- Igneous rocks are formed from magma from the mantle.
- Metamorphic and sedimentary rocks use 'second-hand' materials.
- Sedimentary rocks are formed from other rock types that have been broken down by weathering and erosion.
- Metamorphic rocks are rocks that have been changed by heat and pressure.

Key Point

Think about the effect that rocks have on the UK landscape. The highest areas, igneous and metamorphic, are found in the west and north-west of the UK and the sedimentary rocks are found in the south and south-east.

Flow chart of the rock cycle

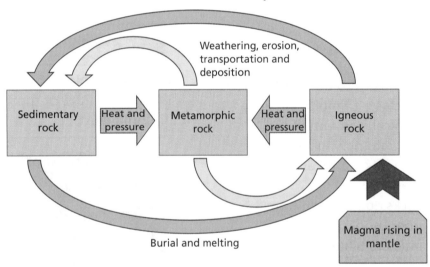

Weathering, erosion, transportation and deposition

Sedimentary rock — Heat and pressure → Metamorphic rock ← Heat and pressure — Igneous rock

Magma rising in mantle

Burial and melting

Igneous rock

Cross-section of the rock cycle

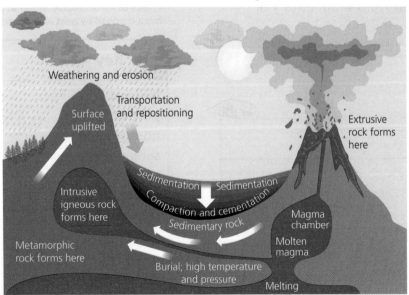

Weathering and erosion

Transportation and repositioning

Surface uplifted

Extrusive rock forms here

Intrusive igneous rock forms here

Sedimentation   Sedimentation

Compaction and cementation

Sedimentary rock

Magma chamber

Molten magma

Metamorphic rock forms here

Burial; high temperature and pressure

Melting

Weathering and Erosion

- All rocks gradually wear away by the action of weather, water, chemicals, plants and animals. This is called **weathering**.
- Weathering involves the interaction of many things, for example, rainfall, temperature and atmospheric gases.
- Weathering produces rock, mineral and chemical debris where the original rock was exposed. Weathering happens in situ (material stays where it is).
- Material produced from weathering is transported by gravity, rivers, sea, ice and wind, before being deposited as sediment.
- The agents of transportation move sediment and also produce more of it. This process is called **erosion**.

Physical Weathering

- Mainly occurs because of the effects of changes in temperature. The presence of water can assist the process.
- The two main types of physical weathering are: freeze-thaw (water freezing in cracks expands and breaks rocks apart) and exfoliation (also known as 'onion-skin weathering'; cracks develop parallel to the land surface as pressure is released, or fast temperature change causes expansion and contraction).

Chemical Weathering

- Occurs as rainwater reacts with minerals to form new minerals. Rainwater is slightly acidic. Higher temperatures aid the process of chemical weathering.
- There are three different types of chemical weathering:
  - Solution – the removal of rock in solution by acidic rainwater.
  - Hydrolysis – acidic water produces clay and salts.
  - Oxidation – rocks broken down by oxygen and water.

Biological Weathering

- Trees put roots through joints and cracks in the rock; the roots eventually break the rocks open.
- Some animals, like limpets, scrape and ingest particles of rock.
- Bacteria and lichens break down the rocks on which they live.
- The burrowing of animals (e.g. rabbits) and birds that nest underground (e.g. puffins) is also classified as biological weathering.

Key Point

Erosion uses a transport agent to remove material and take it elsewhere. Weathering breaks down rock into fragments – no movement is involved.

Key Point

The temperature has to fluctuate (rise and fall) above and below 0°C for freeze-thaw weathering to occur.

Limpets grouped on a cliff

Quick Test

1. Name three things that interact to cause weathering.
2. What happens to water to make it split rocks open?
3. What two substances break down rocks during oxidation?
4. How do trees break open rocks?

Key Words

weathering
erosion

Weathering and Soil 1

You must be able to:

- Describe weathering
- Explain these four processes of weathering: carbonation (chemical weathering); freeze-thaw and onion-skin (physical weathering); and tree roots and burrowing animals (biological weathering).

Weathering

- Weathering is the breakdown of rocks by the action of the weather, plants and animals.

Chemical Weathering

- **Carbonation** takes place when weak acid in rainwater dissolves rocks:
  1. Limestone is made from a mineral called calcium carbonate.
  2. This reacts with weak carbonic acid in rainwater to form soluble minerals.
  3. Dissolved minerals are washed away and the limestone is weathered.

Carbonation

> **Key Point**
>
> Weathering is the breakdown of rocks by the action of the weather, plants and animals. It is different from erosion, which is the removal of the weathered fragments by rivers, glaciers, wind and the sea.

Physical Weathering

- **Freeze-thaw weathering** happens in cold, usually mountainous, locations:
  1. Water gets into cracks in rocks.
  2. The water freezes and expands.
  3. This puts pressure on the rock causing it to split and break up.

Freeze–thaw weathering

- **Onion-skin weathering** occurs in places where there is a significant difference between day and night temperatures, such as in deserts:
  1. During the day the Sun heats the rocks causing them to expand.
  2. During the night the rocks cool down and contract.
  3. The surface of the rocks heats up and cools down faster than the core of the rocks which creates stress and tension in the rock.
  4. Eventually the surface layers of the rock crack and begin to peel away like the outer layers of an onion.

Onion-skin weathering (exfoliation)

| 1 Expansion | 2 Contraction | 3 Rock fractures |

Corestones created by onion-skin weathering

Biological Weathering

- Plant roots can force their way through weaknesses (cracks and joints) in rocks.
- As the plants grow, their roots grow wider and longer, and the rocks are cracked and split apart.
- Animals that burrow into slopes and hedges, for example rabbits, can cause the ground to be weakened and soil and rocks to be broken up as they dig their burrows.
- Birds that nest in cliffs and underground, for example puffins and some terns, can weaken soft cliffs and ground by their digging.

Trees that have taken root in rocks

Quick Test

1. What is weathering?
2. What has to happen to the temperature for freeze-thaw weathering to take place?
3. What does the weather have to be like for onion-skin weathering to take place?

Key Words

carbonation
freeze-thaw weathering
onion-skin weathering

Weathering and Soil 2

You must be able to:

- Understand how soil is formed
- Describe the structure of soil, including the different layers
- Compare soil in the UK with soil in tropical rainforests.

Soil

- Soil is the upper layer of the Earth's surface where plants grow.
- Soil is formed from a mixture of weathered rock and decayed plant and animal matter known as **humus**. Most soils also contain billions of micro-organisms, insects, worms, water and air.
- The factors that influence the formation of soil are:
  - climate: high temperatures increase the rate of soil formation
  - organisms: micro-organisms, insects, worms and plants
  - **parent material**: the type of rock that the soil has been weathered from
  - relief: the shape of the land
  - time.
- Approximately 75 billion tonnes of soil are lost from fields due to soil erosion globally each year, which is equivalent to 100 000 km² of farmland disappearing.
- It can take hundreds of years for 1 cm of soil to form so many people consider soil to be a **non-renewable** resource.
- Farmers are encouraged to reduce soil erosion by planting new hedges (and not removing existing ones) and by ploughing across slopes (contour ploughing) rather than up and down them.

Soil Structure

- Soil can be divided up into several distinct layers or **horizons**:
  - The O horizon is the surface layer consisting of fallen leaves and twigs, animal droppings and dead creatures.
  - The A horizon, or **topsoil**, is the layer of soil directly beneath the surface; it is rich in nutrients, minerals and humus.
  - The B horizon, or **subsoil**, is where the weathered parent rock is becoming soil and nutrients from the topsoil are leached downwards by rainwater.
  - The C horizon is the rock or parent material that the soil has been formed from.
  - The R horizon is the solid **bedrock** at the base of the soil.

Key Point

The formation of soil is affected by climate, organisms, parent material, land relief and time.

Key Point

A non-renewable resource is one that is being used or removed at a faster rate than it is being made.

Soil structure

Soil in the UK

- The soil found in deciduous woods and forests in the UK is known as **brown earth**; it covers 45% of the UK.
- Brown earth is usually 1–2 m deep with a relatively thick layer of topsoil (20 cm on average).
- Brown earth soil is approximately 10 000 years old.

Brown earth

Topsoil

Key Point

Soil is essential for life to survive on the planet. Without soil, plants could not grow, animals would have nothing to eat and, ultimately, humans would not be able to feed themselves.

Soil in Tropical Rainforests

- The soil found in tropical rainforests is known as **latosol**. It has formed over 100 million years and can be 20–30 m deep.
- The topsoil is thin (2–5 cm deep) due to the rapid recycling of nutrients from dead plants and creatures by the forest and the **leaching** of nutrients by heavy rainfall.

A tropical rainforest

Key Words

humus
parent material
non-renewable
horizons
topsoil
subsoil
bedrock
brown earth
latosol
leaching

 Quick Test

1. What is the word for decayed plant and animal matter found in soil?
2. What does topsoil contain?
3. How deep can soils in tropical rainforests become?

Weather and Climate 1

You must be able to:

- Outline the different elements that make up the weather
- Understand how weather is recorded
- Understand why weather changes over time.

What is Weather?

- **Weather** is the daily changes in the atmosphere that affect, and sometimes control, human activity.
- Weather elements include:
  - temperature   – precipitation   – wind
  - humidity   – air pressure.
- **Temperature** tells us how hot or cold the air is at a particular time. Humans are interested in the **minimum** (lowest) **temperature**, the **maximum** (highest) **temperature** and the **temperature range** (the difference between maximum and minimum).
- **Precipitation** is the rainfall, sleet, snow and hail that reaches the ground:
  - Hail is formed from ice pellets, and snow is formed from ice crystals.
  - Sleet is partly melted snow.
- Wind direction affects the temperature of the air. In the UK, winds which come from the north bring cold air and winds blowing from the south bring warmer air. High wind speeds can cause damage to trees and property.
- **Humidity** is the amount of moisture in the air. On damp, foggy days there will be lots of moisture in the air; on hot, sunny days the air may be quite dry.
- **Air pressure** is an important weather element. When warm air rises, the air pressure is reduced (low pressure) and when cold air sinks, the air pressure is increased (high pressure).

Measuring Weather

- In order to make a weather forecast, it is important to collect weather data that shows what is happening now.
- Most modern weather instruments are electronic and connected to computers that are programmed to record and analyse the measurements they take.
- A rain gauge is used to record rainfall, which is measured in millimetres. In south-east England, about 600 mm of rainfall is recorded each year but in the north-west, the figure may be as high as 3000 mm per year.

Key Point

Weather is the daily changes in the atmosphere.

Key Point

The movement of air from areas of high pressure to areas of low pressure causes the wind.

A weather station

- A thermometer is used to record temperature. Temperature is recorded using degrees Celsius (°C) or degrees Fahrenheit (°F). The UK has distinct seasons with colder temperatures in winter (average around 5°C) and hotter temperatures in summer (average around 17°C).
- Wind speed is recorded with an instrument called an anemometer. The units may be mph, m/s or knots.
- Wind direction is recorded with a wind vane that uses compass directions or degrees.
- Air pressure is recorded with a barometer. The units of pressure are called millibars (mbs).
- A weather station may also record the amount and type of clouds in the sky.
- Satellite images can show us detailed pictures of cloud cover over very large areas. Many weather satellites are also fitted with rainfall radar that shows where it is raining.

Weather Forecast

- A daily weather forecast helps us to make decisions about what to wear, what we might eat and where we might go.
- Farmers need forecasts to plan when to sow seeds or harvest crops, and airlines and rail companies need to plan for bad weather.
- A weather forecast for the next 24 hours can be very accurate. It can tell us what the temperature is likely to be, what the risk of rain is and when the rain may arrive at a particular place. It can also predict frost, fog and high winds that may cause problems for people.
- As computers have become more powerful, we can now predict the weather up to a month in advance. Forecast accuracy decreases the further into the future it is.

Why Does the Weather Change?

- The air in our atmosphere is constantly on the move. This is caused by heating by the Sun.
- Once air is warmed, it becomes lighter and rises (think of a hot air balloon). Rising air will eventually cool again, causing clouds to form. These may produce rain or snow.
- Places near the sea are often much wetter as the wind picks up moisture from the sea and carries it over the land.

A storm seen from a satellite

 Key Point

Computers process millions of pieces of data to predict what the weather will do. This is used for weather forecasts.

 Key Point

Solar energy is stronger at the Equator as it is more concentrated. Solar energy is weaker at the poles as it is spread out over a wider area.

 Key Words

weather
minimum temperature
maximum temperature
temperature range
precipitation
humidity
air pressure

Quick Test

1. What is weather?
2. Name three types of precipitation.
3. What does an anemometer measure?

Weather and Climate 2

You must be able to:

- Recognise what a climate graph looks like and how it is constructed
- Understand the differences between the main climate zones that cover the Earth
- Understand why climate varies from place to place.

What is Climate?

- **Climate** is the pattern of average temperature and rainfall data over a year. Data is collected for a minimum of 30 years to get an average.
- The changes in temperature and rainfall can be shown on a **climate graph**. The different parts of the graph show the seasons.
- On a climate graph, rainfall is plotted as a bar graph and temperature is plotted above as a line graph. They share the same *x*-axis, which shows months.
- A climate graph can be used to calculate:
  - maximum temperature
  - temperature range
  - driest month
  - minimum temperature
  - wettest month
  - total annual rainfall.

Climate data for a town in northern England

Range of temperature: 13°C

Total annual rainfall: 810 mm

Types of Climate

- The world is covered by different **climate zones**. These are large areas that share the same pattern of temperature and rainfall.
- The UK, and many parts of Western Europe, has a **temperate climate**. This means summers are cool/warm, winters are cold/mild, and rainfall is moderate.
- In North Africa and the Middle East there is a **desert climate**. This is very hot all year round and has a low total rainfall.
- In the northern part of South America, central Africa and South East Asia, there is a **tropical climate**. This is hot all year round with a high total rainfall.
- The **tundra climate** is found only in the Northern Hemisphere, around the edges of the Arctic Circle. Similar to the **polar climate** of the Arctic and Antarctica, temperatures remain below 0°C for much of the year and there is very little precipitation, which mainly falls as snow.

Factors Affecting Climate

- The climate zones stretch around the world in bands parallel to the lines of latitude. As you travel north from the Equator, you will pass through tropical, then desert, then temperate and finally through tundra and polar climate zones.

> ### Key Point
>
> Climate is the seasonal changes in temperature and rainfall over a year.

Desert climate

Tropical climate

Climate zones

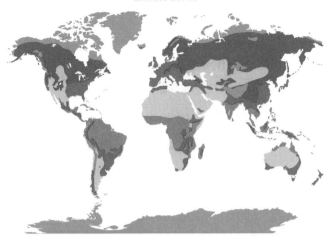

Key:
■ Temperate climate
■ Desert climate
■ Tropical climate
■ Tundra climate
■ Polar climate

Angle of the Sun's rays

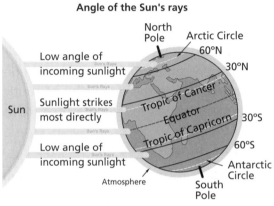

- In general, it gets colder as you move from the Equator to the poles. This is because the energy from the Sun is strongest at the Equator and weakest at the poles.
- In equatorial areas (between the Tropic of Cancer and the Tropic of Capricorn), the Sun is always overhead for part of the year and its energy passes through less of the atmosphere.
- In polar areas, the Sun's energy strikes the Earth at a low angle and so passes through a thicker layer of atmosphere. Some energy is lost by reflection back into space.
- **Altitude** (height above sea level) also affects climate. In mountain areas it is almost always colder, with more rain and snow falling each year when compared with lowland areas.
- The location of a place in relation to the sea affects climate since places near the sea are generally milder and wetter than places that are in the middle of the large continents:
  - In the middle of Russia, it is very hot in summer and very cold in winter.
  - In the UK, which is the same distance from the Equator, it is warm in summer and mild in winter.
- Warm and cold **ocean currents** will also affect places near the coast. The warm waters of the Gulf Stream flow from the Gulf of Mexico towards the UK and make our climate much milder than it would be otherwise in winter.
- The cold waters of the Labrador Current flow south from Greenland towards Canada and make the climate of the entire coast of Canada much colder.
- In California, an offshore cold current causes thick, cold fogs to form along the coast, while inland temperatures may reach 30°C.

Quick Test

1. What two things are shown on a climate graph?
2. Where might we find a tropical climate?
3. What kind of climate do most Middle East countries have?
4. What does the word 'altitude' mean?

> **Key Words**

climate
climate graph
climate zone
temperate climate
desert climate
tropical climate
tundra climate
polar climate
altitude
ocean current

Physical Geography

Glaciation 1

You must be able to:

- Describe what glaciers are and where they are found
- Understand how glaciers form
- Describe how glaciers shape the landscape
- Recognise erosional landforms created by glaciers.

What and Where are Glaciers?

- A glacier is a large moving body of ice that flows slowly due to the force of gravity.
- Ice in the form of glaciers, ice sheets and ice caps covers 10% of the Earth's land area.
- Glaciers can be found at high altitudes in mountain ranges (alpine glaciers) or in the far north and south latitudes of the Arctic and Antarctica where temperatures are low enough for them to form.

 Key Point

20 000 years ago, ice covered most of the UK during the glacial period known as the Pleistocene.

How a Glacier Forms

- Glaciers form where more snow falls each year than can melt; the resulting build up of snow is called **accumulation**.
- Over time, the weight of the accumulated snow causes the layers beneath to become compacted and dense. At this stage it is called **firn**.
- The process of glacier ice formation is very slow and takes hundreds of years.
- The weight of the ice mass causes it to slide and advance downhill due to gravity.
- In warmer months melting, or **ablation**, may take place at the **snout** of the glacier causing it to **retreat**.

Formation of a glacier

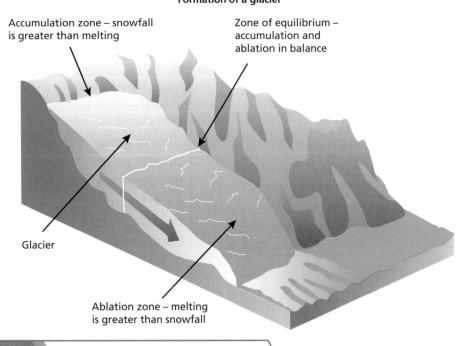

Accumulation zone – snowfall is greater than melting

Zone of equilibrium – accumulation and ablation in balance

Glacier

Ablation zone – melting is greater than snowfall

- Processes of weathering (freeze-thaw) and erosion (plucking and abrasion) carve out the landscape:
  - **Freeze-thaw:** when water freezes and expands in cracks in rock causing it to break apart.
  - **Plucking:** when meltwater at the base and sides of a glacier freezes around rocks, which are then plucked from the landscape as the glacier advances.
  - **Abrasion:** when rocks carried along by the glacier scour and smooth the landscape.

Erosional Landforms

- Corries are hollow-shaped landforms.
  1. After the glacial ice has melted a lake may remain in the corrie. This is known as a tarn (for example, Red Tarn in the Lake District).
  2. Arêtes are knife-like ridges that form when two corries are back to back (for example, Striding Edge in the Lake District).
  3. Pyramidal peaks form when three or more corries form back to back (for example, Stob Dearg in Scotland).
  4. U-shaped valleys are created as the glacier advances. It will widen, deepen and straighten the valley from a V shape to a U shape.
  5. Ribbon lakes are long, narrow lakes that can be found in U-shaped valleys when less resistant rock on the valley floor is eroded more deeply by the glacier (for example, Windermere in the Lake District).
  6. Hanging valleys and waterfalls can be found at the sides of this U-shaped valley. They show how smaller valleys entering the main valley have been cut off by the wide and deep glacier.
  7. Truncated spurs are the cut-off (truncated) hills that once led towards the main valley.

Corrie formation

Quick Test

1. Name the two main processes of glacial erosion.
2. Explain the formation of glacial firn.
3. Describe the shape of a corrie.
4. Describe and explain the formation of a hanging valley.

Key Words

accumulation
firn
ablation
snout
retreat
freeze-thaw
plucking
abrasion

Glaciation 2

You must be able to:

- Describe and explain the formation of depositional landforms
- Explore the problems of managing glacial landscapes
- Define sustainable tourism.

Quick Recall Quiz

Depositional Landforms

- **Moraine** is the name given to the material deposited after a glacier melts:
  - Terminal moraine marks the farthest advance of the glacier.
  - Lateral moraine is deposited along the sides of the glacier.
  - Medial moraine forms where the lateral moraine of two glaciers running side by side is deposited as a ridge along the centre of a valley after melting.
- **Drumlins** are hills shaped like half-buried eggs or teardrops. They are pointed in the direction that the glacier advances. They are often found in groups known as a drumlin field or 'a basket of eggs'.
- Drumlins are formed in this way:
  1 Glacier meets obstruction on valley floor.
  2 Moraine is deposited behind the obstruction.
  3 Glacier moves over obstruction and streamlines it.
  4 The downstream end is tapered by the advancing glacier.
- **Erratics** are large rocks or boulders that may have been transported hundreds of kilometres by a glacier and deposited when it melted.
- Erratics may be a completely different rock type to that found in the area where they are dropped.

Key Point

Drumlins are typically 1–2 km long, less than 50 m in height and around 500 m wide.

Drumlins

Direction of glacier flow

Drumlin

50 m

1.5 km

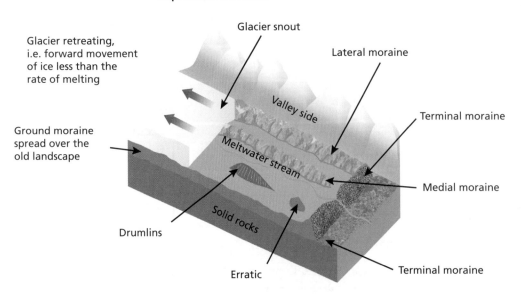

Depositional landforms

Glacier retreating, i.e. forward movement of ice less than the rate of melting

Glacier snout

Lateral moraine

Valley side

Terminal moraine

Ground moraine spread over the old landscape

Meltwater stream

Medial moraine

Drumlins

Solid rocks

Erratic

Terminal moraine

A glacial erratic boulder in North Wales

Managing Glacial Landscapes

- Glacial landscapes are often beautiful areas with dramatic scenery and landforms that attract many tourists. They are often very fragile environments.
- An area that attracts large numbers of tourists is known as a **honeypot** site (e.g. Castleton in the Peak District).
- Glacial landscapes are also home to local people who work, farm or may have retired there.
- Environmentalists and conservationists will be involved in protecting these unique areas.
- If tourism is to be **sustainable** then the impacts on local people, the economy and the environment need to be managed in a balanced way.

Conflict in Glacial Landscapes

- Conflict may arise owing to the different demands of farmers, environmentalists and tourists and needs careful management by local authorities.
- Visitor centres are a good way to begin educating tourists on how to protect these unique landscapes.

Tourist Impact	Problem	Solution
Footpaths overused	Vegetation destroyed; land eroded	Divert popular routes to allow old paths time to recover
Speedboats	Noise and water pollution; erosion	Speed limits Promote sailing
Dog walkers	Disturb cattle	Keep dogs on leads around farms
Traffic	Traffic jams; air and noise pollution	Promote public transport and bike paths
Overcrowding	Traffic congestion and parking; thousands of visitors disturbing locals; landscape congestion	Better public transport Educating visitors to be considerate

A glacial landscape

Key Words

moraine
drumlin
erratic
honeypot
sustainable

Quick Test

1. Describe the shape of a drumlin. Use a diagram if you want to.
2. Why might erratics have a different rock type to the area in which they are found?
3. Explain two ways in which tourist activities might cause problems for local people in a honeypot area.

Review Questions

Location Knowledge – Russia, China, India and the Middle East

1 How cold can it get in the tundra regions of the far north of Russia? [1]

2 a) Define the term 'natural resource'. [2]

    b) Give three examples of high-tech industries found in Russia. [3]

3 What is the capital of China and how many people live there? [2]

4 a) When was the Sichuan earthquake? [2]

    b) How large was the earthquake on the Richter scale? [1]

    c) How many people died in the Sichuan earthquake? [1]

5 What is the land area of the Indo-Gangetic plain? [1]

6 Which is the largest religious group in India? Tick (✓) the correct option.

Sikh	☐	Hindu	☐
Christian	☐	Muslim	☐
Jew	☐	Buddhist	☐

[1]

7 Name four of India's main industries. [4]

8 a) Name two deserts that are found in the Middle East. [2]

    b) How large is the Rub' al-Khali and how high can its sand dunes reach? [2]

9 Which of the following are oil-exporting countries in the Middle East?
Tick (✓) the correct options.

Qatar	☐	Bahrain	☐
Turkey	☐	Kuwait	☐
Israel	☐	Oman	☐

[4]

Africa and Asia Compared – Kenya and South Korea

1 How many times larger is Kenya than the UK? [1]

2 What is Kenya's total annual rainfall and how does this compare to the UK's rainfall? [2]

3 The photo shows montane forest in Kenya. Define the term 'montane forest'. [2]

4 Name South Korea's highest mountain and give its height. [2]

5 Name three types of trees that are found both in the UK and South Korea. [3]

6 What is the life expectancy in South Korea? [1]

7 **a)** When did South Korea achieve independence and from which country? [2]

b) How many people were killed during the civil war between North and South Korea? [1]

Review Questions

Geological Timescale

1   The picture shows a fossil. Which rock type contains fossils?   [1]

2   a) What name is given to the oldest rocks in the UK?   [1]

   b) Where in the UK are these rocks found?   [1]

3   What does the theory of evolution say about which creatures survive over geologic time?   [2]

4   Why did the dinosaurs become extinct?   [2]

5   a) Where in the world did the first humans appear? Tick (✓) the correct option.

   Europe   ☐

   Antarctica ☐

   Africa   ☐

   Asia   ☐   [1]

   b) What are Homo sapiens?   [1]

   c) What is different about the brains of modern humans compared to their ancestors?   [1]

6   Why is it possible that the Earth could get colder rather than warmer in future?   [2]

7   a) How were the chalk rocks found in south-east England formed?   [2]

   b) Why are there ancient desert rocks in central England?   [2]

Plate Tectonics

1 **a)** What is a plate boundary? [1]

b) Name a large mountain range formed at a plate boundary. [1]

c) When two plates move apart at a constructive plate boundary, what fills the gap that is created? [2]

2 Explain why the UK is getting further away from the USA each year. [2]

3 **a)** What is a tsunami? How are they linked to earthquakes? [3]

b) During an earthquake, the ground shakes and cracks. What problems does this cause? [2]

c) Why do many people die in the weeks after an earthquake? [2]

4 What is a hot spot volcano? [2]

5 The photo shows Mount St Helens, a volcano on the west coast of the USA.

a) Why is there a line of volcanoes along the west coast of the USA? [2]

b) Explain why people might want to live near a volcano. [2]

Rocks and Geology

1 **a)** How are igneous rocks formed? [2]

b) Why do some igneous rocks have bigger crystals than others? [4]

2 **a)** What percentage of the Earth's crust is made from metamorphic rocks? [1]

b) Match up the following sedimentary rocks with the metamorphic rocks that they turn into.

Sedimentary   **Metamorphic**

Limestone   Slate

Shale   Marble   [2]

3 Why are some types of rock more likely to contain fossils than others? [2]

4 Study the photograph of the chalk cliffs below. Chalk is a sedimentary rock formed from the shells and skeletons of dead sea creatures.

What evidence is there in the photograph that chalk is a sedimentary rock? [2]

Weathering and Soil

1 **a)** Name an environment where freeze-thaw weathering is likely to take place. [1]

  b) Number these sentences 1–3 to explain how onion-skin weathering takes place.

  A During the night rocks cool down and contract. ☐

  B The surface layers of rock crack and peel away. ☐

  C During the day rocks heat up and expand. ☐ [3]

2 Describe how plants and animals can cause rocks to break up. [2]

3 **a)** Match up the factors that affect the formation of soil with their definitions.

Factors	Definitions
Climate	the type of rock that the soil has weathered from
Organisms	the shape of the land
Parent material	high temperatures increase the rate of soil formation
Relief	insects, worms and plants

[4]

  b) Which factor is missing from the list in question 3a)? [1]

4 How much soil is lost each year from fields due to soil erosion?

Tick (✓) the correct option.

10 billion tonnes ☐

50 billion tonnes ☐

75 billion tonnes ☐

100 billion tonnes ☐ [1]

5 What is the name given to the soil found in tropical rainforests? [1]

Weather and Climate

1 Weather includes temperature, precipitation and air pressure, and which two other elements? [2]

2 Draw lines to match each weather aspect with what it measures.

Minimum temperature		Amount of moisture in the air
Humidity		Amount of moisture that reaches the ground
Precipitation		Lowest temperature recorded each day

[3]

3 What is hail? [1]

4 When air sinks, will this increase or decrease air pressure? [1]

5 What sort of workers might use a weather forecast? Explain how it helps them. [2]

6 When air is warmed by the Sun, what happens to it? [1]

7 Label the two weather elements (A and B) on the climate graph. [2]

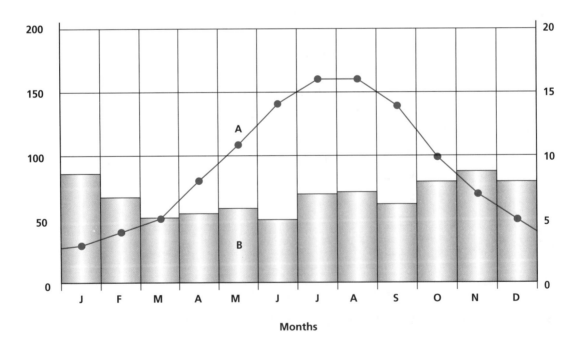

Months

8 Where would you find an equatorial area? [2]

9 What is the Gulf Stream? [3]

Glaciation

1. a) What is a 'glacier'? [2]

   b) What was the Pleistocene? [1]

   c) Describe how glaciers are formed using the following key terms:

      accumulation   compacted   firn   advance   gravity [5]

2. Name the three main processes of glacial weathering and erosion. [3]

3. Name the three types of moraine labelled below:

[3]

4. Fill in the missing words from the description of drumlin formation.

   a) Glacier meets _____ on valley floor.

   b) Moraine is _____ behind the obstruction.

   c) Glacier moves over obstruction and _____ it.

   d) The downstream end is tapered by the _____ glacier. [4]

5. Explain three ways in which tourism can have a negative impact on glacial landscapes. [6]

Rivers and Coasts 1

You must be able to:

- Explain key processes and landforms
- Describe the features found along the river's course
- Understand how people interact with these environments.

Quick Recall Quiz

Rivers

- Rivers flow from source to mouth, passing through three main stages: upper, middle and lower.
- Main features at each stage:

Stage	Dominant Processes	Landforms
Upper	Erosion	V-shaped valley, rapids, waterfalls, gorges
Middle	Erosion and deposition	Meanders, ox-bow lakes
Lower	Deposition	Floodplains and levées

- Three main processes take place in rivers and coastal zones.
  1. **Erosion** is a high energy process in which material is worn away.
  2. **Transportation** is the process by which eroded material is carried away.
  3. **Deposition** is a low energy process in which transported material is deposited.

> ### Key Point
>
> These main processes will work together to form specific landforms.

Parts of a river system

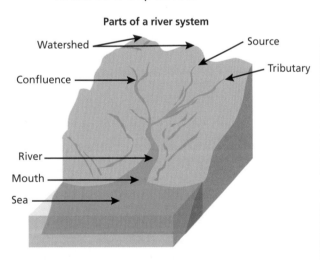

Watershed
Source
Confluence
Tributary
River
Mouth
Sea

Transportation

Solution – dissolved minerals
Suspension – silt
River flow
Traction – boulders
Saltation – pebbles

Erosional Processes

- The key erosional processes are:
  1. **Corrasion** (or abrasion) is the erosion of river beds and banks by rocks carried by the water.
  2. **Attrition** is the process by which rocks become smaller and rounder over time as they repeatedly crash into each other.

Slightly acidic water can erode some types of rock in river beds and banks by dissolving them in a solution.

 Hydraulic action is the erosion of river beds and banks owing to the sheer force of water power.

Landform Formation

- **Waterfalls** – formed through vertical erosion of alternating bands of resistant and less resistant rock; undercutting; plunge pool formation; the waterfall retreats and a steep gorge forms.
- **Meanders** – lateral erosion on outside bend, with deposition on inside bend; bend increases in sinuosity (tighter bends) over time.
- **Floodplains** and **levées** – caused by deposition during river floods; the coarsest material builds up on banks to form levées. Finer silts are deposited from the channel onto floodplains.

Flooding

- A river will flood when water flows into the channel faster than it can be carried downstream. It will overflow its banks and spread out on to the surrounding floodplains.
- Rivers can be managed to try to create a long-term solution to flooding impacts:
  - **Hard engineering** involves using artificial materials to alter the natural flow of the river; in other words, working against nature.
  - **Soft engineering** involves using natural measures to reduce flood risk, e.g. afforestation; in other words, working with nature.
- Physical and human factors contribute to flooding:

Physical	Human
Heavy rain	Urbanisation
Steep slopes	Deforestation
Impermeable rock	Climate change
Many tributaries	
Saturated soil	

Area at risk of flooding

> **Key Point**
>
> Soft engineering is viewed as a more sustainable approach to river management.

> **Key Point**
>
> All of these factors will cause rainwater to flow overland to the river channel. This is the quickest route for water to reach the channel.

> **Key Words**
>
> erosion
> transportation
> deposition
> waterfall
> meander
> floodplain
> levée
> hard engineering
> soft engineering

Quick Test

1. What are the four processes of erosion at work in a river?
2. What is deposition?
3. Which process must be present for the formation of floodplains and levées?

Rivers and Coasts 2

You must be able to:

- Describe the formation of waves
- Explain the formation of coastal landforms
- Consider approaches to coastal management.

Coasts

- Coasts are the narrow zone between the sea and the land.
- Coastal zones are under constant attack from waves and weather.
- Rates of weathering and erosion will vary depending on the rock type of the coast.
- **Differential erosion** creates distinct landforms and **discordant** coastlines with bays and headlands, e.g. Swanage Bay in Dorset.
- Characteristics of discordant coastlines are:

Headlands	Bays
Hard rock, e.g. chalk	Soft rock, e.g. clay
Waves hit headland with force	Waves refracted into bays
Caves, arches, stacks, stumps	Beaches

Wave Formation

- Wind blowing over the surface of the sea transfers energy to the water by friction.
- This energy transfer sets up a circular motion in the water, like rollers on a conveyor belt.
- Wave energy is transferred forward in the direction of the prevailing wind – the water itself does not move forward.
- As a wave reaches the shore, the bottom of the 'roller' meets the sea floor. Friction between the water and the sea floor causes the wave height to increase.
- The top of the wave moves faster than the bottom and the wave topples over as a breaker.

Erosional and Depositional Landforms

- Caves, arches, stacks and stumps are formed in the following way:
  1. Destructive waves attack the exposed headland.
  2. Weaknesses in the headland become cracks and in time caves are formed.
  3. Continued erosion from beneath and **weathering** from above creates an **arch**.
  4. The roof of the arch collapses to leave a **stack**.
  5. The stack decreases in size into a **stump**.

Key Point

Energy within a wave is transferred forward.

Discordant coastline — bays and headlands

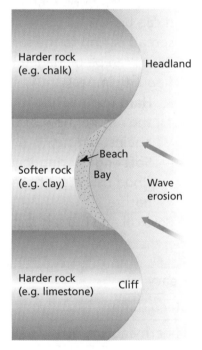

Destructive waves

Backwash more powerful than swash

Constructive waves

Swash more powerful than backwash

- Wave-cut platforms are formed in this way:
  1. At high tide waves attack the base of the cliff.
  2. A **wave-cut notch** forms.
  3. Weathering from above, and further undercutting of the cliff, causes the cliff to collapse.
  4. The sea removes collapsed material.
  5. The process repeats, and the cliff retreats.
  6. A smooth **wave-cut platform** is revealed at low tide.
- Once eroded, material (sediment) is transported along the coastline in the direction of the prevailing wind via the zig-zag movement of **longshore drift**.
- Sand is carried up the beach at an angle (swash) and returns down the beach in a straight line (backwash).

Wave-cut platform

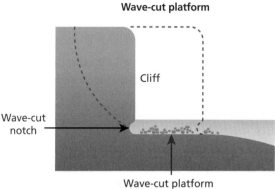

Cliff

Wave-cut notch

Wave-cut platform

Longshore drift

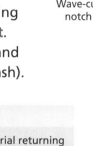

Material returning with backwash directly down slope of beach

Material carried along beach

Slope of beach

Sediment carried up beach by the swash

Dominant waves approach at an angle to the beach

How People Manage Coasts

- Decisions about how to manage the coast can lead to conflict between people with different interests. Residents, tourists, environmentalists, local and national government may all have opposing views.
- Hard and soft engineering strategies can reduce the impact of destructive waves and the loss of sand via longshore drift.

Hard Engineering	Soft Engineering
Curved sea wall – deflects destructive waves	Beach nourishment – ensures wide beach
Rock armour – breaks up wave energy	Dune nourishment – planting marram grass to hold sand dunes together
Groynes – slow longshore drift	Managed retreat – coast left to retreat
Offshore reef – waves break offshore	

Quick Test

1. Which two elements will lead to coastal erosion?
2. Where do waves get their energy from?
3. What is the process by which sand is transported along the coast?
4. Which group of people may prefer soft engineering approaches?

Key Words

differential erosion
discordant
weathering
arch
stack
stump
wave-cut notch
wave-cut platform
longshore drift

Landscapes 1

Quick Recall Quiz

You must be able to:

- Consider the ways in which people interact with natural landscapes
- Understand how these interactions may contribute to climate change
- Understand how these interactions may contribute to desertification.

People and the Earth

- The world's population had grown to nearly 8 billion by 2021.
- Human activities have had an impact on more than 80% of the Earth's land surface.
- The impact of human activity began to increase with the shift to agriculture around 10 000 years ago.
- The built landscape is increasing at a rapid rate as cities, towns and transport technologies grow.
- The natural landscape is exploited by humans as a source of raw materials and energy:
  - Trees and vegetation are removed to make space for farms and cities.
  - Mines and quarries are dug for **natural resources**.
  - Rivers are controlled to provide electricity.
  - Fumes and emissions from transport and factories have a negative impact on the atmosphere.
  - Oceans, rivers and lakes suffer from pollution and overfishing.
- As populations grow, so too does the demand for space and resources, which leads to more fragile landscapes being exploited.
- How humans use, modify and change landscapes may not be **sustainable**.

> **Key Point**
>
> Humans have interacted with the landscape for thousands of years, but with an increasing population comes an increasing demand for resources and land. This can lead to the destruction of natural landscapes.

Crowded city street

People and Rainforests

- Tropical rainforests cover less than 5% of the Earth's surface and play a vital role in the Earth's ecosystem.
- In 2020 there were an estimated 390 billion trees in the Amazon rainforest.
- There may be as many as 5 million species in the world's rainforests, of which only about 10% are known to science.
- As population grows, the demand for wood, resources and land increases. This means that rainforests are being exploited and cleared, resulting in **deforestation**.

Deforestation

- Deforestation results in soil erosion as soils become exposed to rain.
- Nutrients are leached from the soil, resulting in loss of vegetation, leading to a decline in wildlife.

Deforestation and Climate Changes

- With fewer trees, less moisture is evaporated back into the atmosphere.
- This means less rainfall and more drought conditions.
- Trees act as '**carbon sinks**', taking carbon dioxide out of the atmosphere.
- Burning the rainforests releases carbon dioxide into the atmosphere.
- Carbon dioxide is one of the **greenhouse gases** that contribute to global warming.

People and Savannah Grasslands

- Savannah grasslands form on the fringes of rainforests and towards desert margins where there is insufficient rainfall to support forests.
- As population increases, people are exploiting these fragile landscapes.
- This leads to **desertification** as overgrazing by cattle and overcultivation results in soil erosion, leading to an increasing amount of land turning into desert.
- Savannah landscapes are also under threat as global warming causes deserts to expand into them.
- Desert environments are fragile with a low **carrying capacity**.
- Carrying capacity is the maximum number of people that the land can support.

Animals roaming across savannah grassland

Key Point

Climate change is also responsible for increased dry periods and less rainfall.

Desertification

- Results from a combination of physical processes and human activity.
- Land becomes infertile and unproductive.
- It is a serious problem in the Sahel region of Africa where many countries meet the edges of the Sahara Desert.
- Affects some of the poorest people in the world.

Quick Test

1. Why are fragile landscapes exploited?
2. Why are rainforests described as 'carbon sinks'?
3. Where do savannah grasslands form?
4. Define the term 'desertification'.

Key Words

natural resources
sustainable
deforestation
carbon sink
greenhouse gases
desertification
carrying capacity

Landscapes 2

Quick Recall Quiz

You must be able to:

- Understand how indigenous people live in rainforests
- Consider how indigenous people are important in fragile landscapes
- Explore sustainable strategies to prevent soil erosion in savannah landscapes.

Indigenous People in Rainforests

- There are many **indigenous** people, such as the Yanomamo in the Amazon rainforest of Brazil, who have lived in the tropical rainforests for thousands of years.
- It is important to understand that indigenous people have much to teach us about rainforests.
- They are hunter-gatherers, finding food, clothing and housing from the forest.
- Indigenous people move their villages regularly to allow the landscape to recover and grow back.
- They live a sustainable existence because they use the land without destroying the environment.
- Indigenous populations are decreasing because:
  - their homes are being destroyed by deforestation
  - they are killed by introduced diseases, such as measles, for which they have no resistance
  - they are forced into cities by governments who claim to own their land.

An indigenous settlement

Working with Indigenous People

- By working with indigenous people we can learn important information about rainforests, such as their ecology, medicinal plants, food and other products.

> **Key Point**
>
> Humans have interacted with the landscape for thousands of years, but with an increasing population comes an increasing demand for resources and land. This can lead to the destruction of natural landscapes.

A member of an indigenous group

> **Key Point**
>
> Indigenous people can be employed to educate investors about the environment.

- Indigenous people can teach valuable lessons about managing rainforests sustainably.
- It is crucial to realise that they have a right to practise their own lifestyle and to live upon the land where their ancestors have lived before them.

Sustainable Management

Rainforests

- **Reafforestation** by planting trees to replace the ones cut down.
- Selective logging by removing old or diseased trees to make way for younger, healthier ones.
- Conservation by creating protected areas of rainforest.
- **Agroforestry** by planting crops alongside trees rather than cutting them down.
- Satellite photography can be used to monitor illegal deforestation and disruption to indigenous people.

Savannah Grasslands

- Reduce grazing so plants have the chance to grow again and so prevent **soil erosion** and desertification.
- Circles of stones ('magic stones') placed on the ground to hold water on the soil and prevent run-off.
- Planting trees provides shelter from the wind.
- Mulching by adding layers of leaves or straw can reduce evaporation and add nutrients to the soil.
- **Terracing** prevents soil from being washed down slopes when it rains.
- Drought-resistant plants can be used to stabilise the soil.

Terracing prevents soil from being washed down slopes

Key Point

Soil erosion is a result of both natural processes and the way people use the land. Careful management can help reduce the risk of soil erosion and desertification.

Key Point

People across the world can reduce the pressure on deforestation for agriculture by eating less meat and products with palm oil in them.

Key Words

indigenous
reafforestation
agroforestry
soil erosion
terracing

Quick Test

1. How do indigenous people survive in rainforests?
2. How can indigenous people help manage rainforests?
3. What is reafforestation?
4. What are 'magic stones'?

Population 1

Quick Recall Quiz

You must be able to:

- Understand how world population is changing
- Understand where people live in the world
- Explain why some areas have many people and others have few.

World Population

- The world's population was estimated to be 7.9 billion in 2021.
- About 140 million babies are born each year. The number of babies born per 1000 people per year is called the **birth rate**.
- About 55 million people die each year. The number of people dying per 1000 people per year is called the **death rate**.
- Before 1800, birth and death rates roughly balanced each other out and there was little **population growth**.
- Over the last 150 years, however, the rate of population growth has gradually increased – some people call this a 'population explosion'.
- Birth rates are now falling in most parts of the world and so the total world population may level out at around 10 billion people.

Key Point

Geographers and others are worried that there may not be sufficient resources (food, water, minerals, etc.) for the world's growing population.

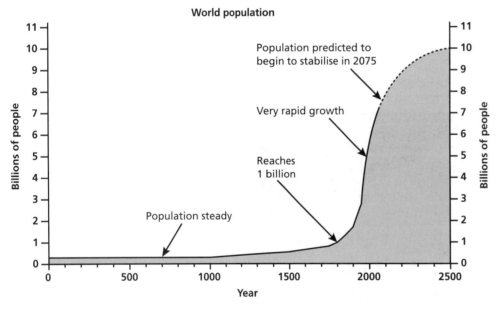

Population Distribution

- **Population distribution** means where people live.
- A **sparse population** (few people) occurs in areas where it is difficult to live (deserts, mountains, marshes and very cold environments) owing to a lack of natural resources.
- Areas with a sparse population include the Sahara Desert, the Himalayas and the Arctic.

- A **dense population** (lots of people) is found in areas where humans can locate most of the things they need (land suitable for building, fertile soil for farming, mineral resources and water).
- Areas with a dense population include most of Western Europe, the eastern USA and large parts of South East Asia.
- In some countries where there are valuable mineral resources, such as oil, people use their wealth and modern technology to create artificial environments. Examples include:
  – Alaska (very cold) in the USA
  – Dubai (very hot and dry) in the Middle East.

Key Point

The number of people living in different parts of the world depends mainly on the climate (average temperature/rainfall) and the resources available.

Population Density

- **Population density** is used to measure the number of people in an area (number of people per square kilometre, for example).
- Although population density is an average figure, it allows us to compare how crowded countries are. It is important to remember that even in crowded countries there may be areas with only a few people.
- A country with a very high population density is Bangladesh, where there are an average 1141 people per square kilometre. The Netherlands (520 people per square km), South Korea (518) and the UK (277) also have relatively high population densities. By comparison, lower population densities are found in China (149), South Africa (49), Peru (25) and Russia (8).
- In the UK, the most crowded place is London with a population density of about 5700 people per square kilometre. The Highlands of Scotland, by comparison, have a population density of about 8 people per square kilometre.

World population density

| 0–10 |
| 10–25 |
| 25–50 |
| 50–75 |
| 75–100 |
| 100–150 |
| 150–300 |
| 300–1000 |
| 1000+ |

Quick Test

1. Roughly how many 'extra people' are there in the world each year?
2. If the world population continues to grow, why may this be a problem in some areas?
3. Why do few people live in very cold or very dry areas?
4. Why is the population density in most of Europe very high?

Key Words

birth rate
death rate
population growth
population distribution
sparse population
dense population
population density

Population 2

You must be able to:

- Explain why people move
- Understand how and why population changes
- Understand population problems.

Population Migration

- When people move from one place to another, this is known as **migration**:
  - The people choosing to leave a country are known as **emigrants**.
  - The people arriving in a new country are called **immigrants**.
- There are laws controlling migration and if people enter a country without permission, they are referred to as illegal immigrants.
- The majority of people who move are economic migrants, seeking higher paid work and a better life.
- If people are forced to leave a country because of famine, war or a natural disaster, they become **refugees**. Many countries such as the UK have special agreements to help refugees start a new life.

Population Change

- If there are more births than deaths in a country, there will be a natural population increase.
- If there are more immigrants than emigrants, there will be a population increase due to migration.
- In the low income countries (LICs) there have been, until recently, very high rates of natural population increase. As the birth rates fall, however, they begin to match the death rates more closely and population growth slows down.
- In the high income countries (HICs) birth and death rates are roughly the same so there is little natural population change each year.

Country	Birth Rate	Death Rate
Denmark	11.0	9.9
UK	11.3	9.4
India	17.1	7.3
Saudi Arabia	16.2	3.6
Ethiopia	30.7	6.1

Population change

*Rates are given per 1000

> ### Key Point
>
> The number of people living in a country can change naturally or through migration, or a combination of the two.

Some cities continue to experience rapid population growth

- Birth rates may be high for many different reasons, including:
  - religious beliefs
  - a lack of contraception
  - in the poorest countries many infants die before they are a year old so people have large numbers of children to compensate.
- In some countries, the government may try to persuade people to have fewer babies through **family planning** campaigns.
- In the poorest countries, high death rates are caused by **poverty**, a lack of food, disease and poor medical care.
- In the richest countries, death rates may still be high due to lack of exercise and poor diet leading to high rates of obesity, cancer and heart disease.

Population Issues

- A rapidly growing population may mean a country doesn't have sufficient resources to provide for the needs of all the people. The **quality of life** for the majority of people may then be low. A few countries in Africa are still in this difficult situation.
- An ageing population (many people over the age of 60 years) is a problem for some of the HICs. A good quality of life and good medical care mean that large numbers of people are living longer.
- An **ageing population** may not have enough people of **working age** to do all the jobs and the older people may need lots of special help and care, which can be very expensive.
- Countries that receive large numbers of refugees fleeing from war and disasters may struggle to provide food, shelter and medical care.
- In the 27 countries of the European Union, people are allowed to migrate freely from one country to another. Many people migrate from the poorer countries of Eastern Europe (e.g. Romania, Bulgaria) to the richer countries of Western Europe, such as Germany, where there are better paid jobs – and this can sometimes cause unrest.

Refugee camp

> **Quick Test**
>
> 1. What is the difference between emigrants and immigrants?
> 2. Why do refugees need help?
> 3. Calculate the difference between the birth and death rates for the UK and for India.
> 4. Why are death rates still quite high in countries such as the USA and the UK?

> **Key Words**
>
> migration
> emigrants
> immigrants
> refugees
> family planning
> poverty
> quality of life
> ageing population
> working age

Urbanisation 1

You must be able to:

- Define the term 'urbanisation'
- Explain the causes of urbanisation
- Understand the characteristics and effects of urbanisation in the UK.

What is Urbanisation?

- **Urbanisation** is the process by which the proportion of people living in urban areas grows. This will happen when more people move to live and work in towns and cities than remain in the countryside.
- **High income countries (HICs)**, such as the UK, USA and Germany, have experienced urbanisation since the 19th century and are now considered to be urbanised.
- **Low income countries (LICs)**, such as Nigeria and Kenya, are experiencing rapid urbanisation today.

> ### Key Point
>
> The more urbanised a country is, the more developed it becomes. The UN predicts that by 2050, 68% of the world's population will live in urban environments.

Causes of Urbanisation

- Causes of urbanisation include:
  - **rural-to-urban migration**: the movement of people from countryside (rural) to towns and cities (urban)
  - **natural increase**: the number of births is greater than the number of deaths.

Poor conditions and a lack of opportunities can push people away from rural life

Push and pull factors leading to rural-to-urban migration

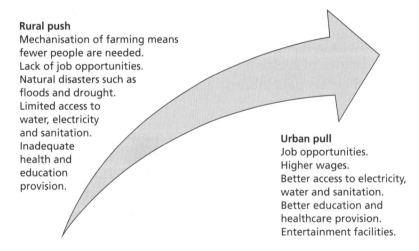

Rural push
Mechanisation of farming means fewer people are needed.
Lack of job opportunities.
Natural disasters such as floods and drought.
Limited access to water, electricity and sanitation.
Inadequate health and education provision.

Urban pull
Job opportunities.
Higher wages.
Better access to electricity, water and sanitation.
Better education and healthcare provision.
Entertainment facilities.

The attractions of the city can pull people towards urban life

Urbanisation in HICs

- During the Industrial Revolution (18th to early 20th century), UK cities grew as manufacturing industries provided jobs and opportunities.

- The proportion of the UK population living in urban areas grew steadily:
  - 1700: 17%
  - 1800: 26%
  - 1900: 77%
  - 2000: 79%
  - Today: 84%
- **Suburbanisation** took place from the 1950s onwards as cities spread and grew outwards.
- Pollution and overcrowding in city centres meant people wanted to live further away.
- Improvements in technology, such as transport infrastructure, increased car ownership and telecommunications meant people could commute more easily or even work away from the urban centre.
- **Counterurbanisation** took place from the 1980s onwards as some people started to move out of cities to surrounding smaller towns and villages.

Examples of suburban and village settlements in the UK

Effects of Recent Urban Processes in HICs

- Increase in population and employment away from city centres.
- Large edge-of-town shopping centres attract people from suburbs and beyond.
- Inner cities suffer from derelict factories, abandoned shops, poor quality housing, unemployment, crime.
- **Urban decline** became a problem across the UK. For example, the decline of the London Docklands from the 1950s as large container ships could no longer access the port resulted in rising unemployment, poverty and poor quality housing.

Response to Urban Decline in the UK

- **Urban regeneration** projects were initiated in many UK cities in an attempt to attract people and businesses back to the cities.
- The London Docklands Development Corporation was set up in 1981 to attract new businesses, money and people to the area:
  - Abandoned warehouses were converted into flats and apartments.
  - The Docklands Light Railway improved links to the rest of London.
  - The Millennium Dome (now the O2 Arena) was built to provide entertainment and leisure attractions.
  - A shopping centre was built close to Canary Wharf.

Redeveloped London Docklands

Quick Test

1. Define the term 'urbanisation'.
2. Explain how push and pull factors lead to urbanisation.
3. Explain the causes of suburbanisation.
4. Why did UK cities need regeneration projects?

 Key Words

urbanisation
high income countries (HICs)
low income countries (LICs)
rural-to-urban migration
suburbanisation
counterurbanisation
urban decline
urban regeneration

Urbanisation 2

You must be able to:

- Understand the characteristics and effects of urbanisation in LICs
- Recognise the difference between HICs' and LICs' experience of urbanisation
- Explain the importance of sustainable urban management.

Urbanisation in LICs

- Lower income countries (LICs) have experienced rapid growth of urban populations since the 1950s; for example, in China the urban population grew from 13% in 1950 to 63.9% in 2020.
- A **megacity** is defined as a city with a population greater than 10 million. By 2025 it is estimated that there will be 35 megacities in LICs.
- LIC cities struggle to provide housing, services and jobs to meet the needs of their expanding populations.
- New arrivals are forced to live in makeshift housing on unwanted land around the city.
- These slum areas are known as '**shanty towns**' ('favelas' in Brazil and 'bustees' in India).
- Despite the poor living conditions, they are often described as hopeful and active places where everything is recycled imaginatively. Dharavi, a large slum in Mumbai, India, has over 300 000 'rag-pickers' who collect and recycle 80 per cent of Mumbai's waste.
- Local communities, charities and governments are working to help improve the quality of living in shanty towns.

> **Key Point**
>
> Unlike the steady growth of HIC cities over 200 years, LIC cities have grown rapidly in just 60 years, making it difficult for governments to provide sufficient homes and services.

Lack of water supply, electricity, sewage system

Makeshift housing

Lack of waste disposal

Unwanted land

Poor roads and access

Effects of rapid urbanisation in LICs – shanty towns

- The grassroots approach involves the shanty town inhabitants in the planning process and has proved to be very successful.
- **Self-help schemes** give local people ownership of their land and provide them with training and tools to improve their homes themselves.
- Local authorities often try to improve living conditions by providing improved access to electricity, clean water and sanitation alongside improving refuse collection, paving roads, etc.

Sustainable Urban Management

- Many people are working towards trying to make cities more sustainable.
- A **sustainable city** offers a good quality of life to current residents but doesn't reduce the opportunities for future residents.
- Society (people), the economy (money) and the environment must all be considered equally. Making cities more sustainable includes strategies such as providing affordable housing, improving air quality, reducing traffic congestion and increasing provision of green space.

A sustainable city

Energy efficient homes (i.e. with solar panels/well insulated)

Open green spaces

Street lighting makes cities safer

Recycling bins

Traffic calming in roads

Bus and bike lanes

Walking and cycling is safe – pedestrianised streets

> ## Quick Test
>
> 1. What is the major difference between the experience of urbanisation for HICs and LICs?
> 2. Describe a 'shanty town'.
> 3. What is meant by the term 'grassroots approach'?
> 4. What three things must be considered if a city is to be managed sustainably?

> ### Key Point
>
> Sustainable cites require the committed support of governments and the active participation of the public to be successful.

> ### Key Words
>
> **megacity**
> **shanty town**
> **self-help scheme**
> **sustainable city**

Review Questions

Rocks and Geology

1 Define the term 'porous rock'. [1]

2 **a) i)** What are sedimentary rocks made from? [2]

  ii) Name three sedimentary rocks. [3]

  b) i) Which two processes are required for metamorphic rocks to form? [2]

  ii) Name three metamorphic rocks. [3]

3 What is the difference between intrusive and extrusive rocks? [2]

4 Study the diagram of the formation of sedimentary rocks.

Match the processes from the list below with the lettered places on the diagram.

Processes

Particles build up in layers. ———

Over millions of years new rock
forms on the seabed. ———

Particles sink to the bottom of
the sea. ———

Eroded particles transported by rivers
to the sea. ——— [4]

5 Study the photograph of Hay Tor in Dartmoor in the UK. Hay Tor is made from granite, which is an igneous rock.

Explain how igneous rocks are formed.

[4]

Weathering and Soil

1 Name the mineral in limestone and the acid in rainwater that react together during chemical weathering. [2]

2 Number these statements **1–3** to explain the process of freeze-thaw weathering.

Water freezes and expands. ☐

Water gets into cracks in rocks. ☐

Rocks split and break up. ☐ [3]

3 Why does repeated heating and cooling cause the surface of rocks to split and flake off when onion-skin weathering takes place? [4]

4 What is the difference between weathering and erosion? [2]

5 **a)** What is 'contour ploughing' and what does it aim to achieve? [2]

b) Why do some people describe soil as a non-renewable resource? [1]

c) Give three factors that affect the rate of soil erosion. [3]

6 Describe three characteristics of brown earth. [3]

7 **a)** How much of the UK is covered by brown earth? Tick (✓) the correct answer.

10% ☐

25% ☐

45% ☐

65% ☐ [1]

b) How old is brown earth soil? Tick (✓) the correct answer.

1000 years ☐

10 000 years ☐

100 000 years ☐

1 million years ☐ [1]

Review Questions

Weather and Climate

1 Which of the following are types of solid precipitation?

Tick (✓) the correct options.

Hail ☐

Rain ☐

Snow ☐ [2]

2 a) How does wind direction affect the weather in the UK? [1]

b) Why do people worry about high wind speeds in the weather forecast? [1]

3 If a rain gauge measured a total rainfall for the year of about 600 mm, in which part of the UK would it be most likely to be located?

Tick (✓) the correct option.

North-west England ☐

South-east England ☐ [1]

4 On a foggy day, is humidity likely to be high or low? [1]

5 Which will be more accurate and why?

Tick (✓) the correct option, then give your reason.

A weather forecast for the next 24 hours ☐

A weather forecast for the next 30 days ☐ [2]

6 In the UK, how much hotter is the average temperature in summer than in winter? [3]

7 a) Put the following climate zones in the correct order as you travel from the North Pole to the Equator:

   tundra   desert   temperate   polar   tropical [4]

b) What sort of temperature and rainfall pattern would be found in a tropical climate? [2]

8 Why is some of the Sun's energy lost by reflection near the North and South poles? [2]

Glaciation

1 What does accumulation mean? [2]

2 When will ablation take place? [2]

3 Lakes often form in glacial troughs. The photograph shows an example of this.

What is the name given to this type of lake? [1]

4 Where are tarns found? [2]

5 Give the names of features A, B and C in the following diagram. B and C are types of valley. [3]

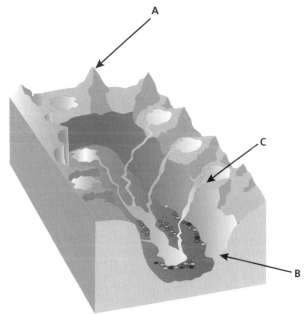

6 What is moraine? [2]

7 Explain how an erratic can be identified. [2]

8 What is a honeypot site? [3]

9 **a)** Name three groups of people who interact in glacial landscapes. [3]

b) How can dog walkers cause a problem in glacial landscapes? [4]

c) Why are visitor centres important in the protection of glacial landscapes? [4]

Rivers and Coasts

1 Name the three processes that take place to shape the landscape around rivers and coasts. [3]

2 Describe the erosional process of corrasion (abrasion). [2]

3 Name one common landform found in the upper course of a river. [1]

4 Name the feature at X below and identify the processes occurring at A and B. [3]

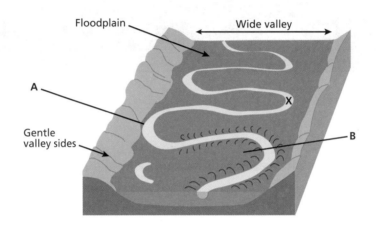

5 Explain what causes a river to flood. [2]

6 Describe the formation of waves. [5]

7 Name features A and B on the diagram below. [2]

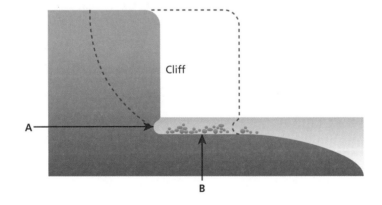

8 Give one advantage and one disadvantage of hard engineering. [2]

Landscapes

1 The photograph shows a built-up city landscape.

   Why is the built landscape of the world increasing?   [2]

2 Give three ways in which humans exploit natural landscapes.   [3]

3 Name one tropical rainforest and outline why it is such an important ecosystem.   [3]

4 a) Describe how indigenous people live sustainably in rainforests.   [4]

   b) Give three reasons to suggest why indigenous populations are decreasing.   [3]

   c) Explain why working with indigenous people can lead to sustainable management
      of rainforests.   [5]

5 Explain how the land in savannah grasslands can be managed to reduce the risk of
   desertification.   [6]

Population

1. The graph shows the actual and predicted world population.

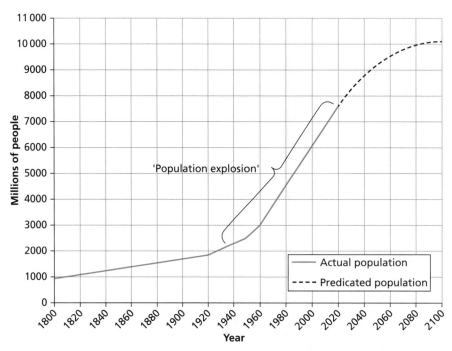

   a) According to the graph, what was the world population in 2020? [1]

   b) Why is the present growth rate sometimes called a 'population explosion'? [2]

   c) What is the world population likely to be in around 100 years? [1]

2. Explain the difference between a 'sparse' population and a 'dense' population. [2]

3. Why do more people than expected live in harsh environments such as Alaska in the USA? [1]

4. Name one country with a high population density and one country with a low population density. [2]

5. What is the difference between a refugee and an illegal immigrant? [2]

6. What causes 'natural' population increase in a country? [1]

7. What is a family planning campaign? [2]

8. Describe one problem resulting from a country having an ageing population. [2]

Urbanisation

1. **a)** Define the process of urbanisation. [2]

    b) What are the two main causes of urbanisation? [4]

    c) Explain why the mechanisation of farming contributes to urbanisation. [3]

2. What is the difference between suburbanisation and counterurbanisation? [3]

3. **a)** Explain why inner cities have experienced decline. [4]

    b) Using an example of an urban regeneration project that you have studied, describe
two of its aims. [2]

4. What is the key difference between HICs' and LICs' experience of urbanisation? [2]

5. **a)** Which of the following are typical characteristics of shanty towns?
Tick (✓) the correct options.

    No electricity ☐

    Spacious living conditions ☐

    Running water ☐

    Lack of roads ☐

    Corrugated iron roofs ☐

    Sewage system ☐

    No waste disposal ☐ [4]

    b) Explain the aims of self-help schemes as an approach to improving shanty towns. [4]

6. Study the images below and list the features that characterise a sustainably planned city. [6]

Development 1

You must be able to:

- Define the term 'development'
- Identify indicators that measure development
- Consider factors that slow down the development process
- Identify the location of developed and developing countries.

What is Development?

- Development measures how different countries compare to each other in terms of economic, social, technological, cultural and environmental factors.
- High levels of development lead to an improved standard of living and quality of life.
- High income countries (HICs) are often referred to as *developed* and low income countries (LICs) as *developing*.

Measuring Development

- Different **indicators** can be used to measure and compare levels of development in different countries:

Examples of Social Indicators	Examples of Economic Indicators
• Birth rate: the number of babies born per thousand people per year. • Life expectancy: the average age a person will live to. • Infant mortality rates: the number of babies who die before their first birthday measured per thousand live births. • Literacy rates: the percentage of the population who can read and write. • The percentage of people living in urban areas. • Access to clean water: the percentage of the total population that can access safe drinking water.	• Gross Domestic Product (GDP): the total value of a country's goods and services in one year. • GDP per capita (per person): the GDP divided by the total population of a country. • The percentage of people working in the primary sector (raw materials: farming, mining, fishing), secondary sector (manufacturing), tertiary sector (services) and quaternary sector (information).

> **Key Point**
>
> NIC means newly industrialising country. These are countries such as India and China that have rapidly developing economies.

Why are some Countries Slower to Develop?

- There are human and physical factors that have a negative impact on the development process in many countries.
- Examples of human factors:
  - Past colonial activities stripped many LICs of their resources (to the benefit of the colonial powers).
  - Poor governance may mean that money is held by a few powerful people and not used to develop the health, education and employment of the population.
  - Disease affects people's ability to work or go to school.
  - LICs' exports are mainly primary produce, which is of a lower value than the goods they import from HICs, leading to a **trade deficit**.
  - HICs control the price they pay LICs for their primary produce.
  - Many LICs have borrowed money from HICs so much of their GDP is spent paying off the **debt**.
- Examples of physical factors:
  - Many countries (e.g. those in sub-Saharan Africa) suffer from conditions like drought, which leaves soils infertile and unproductive.
  - Natural disasters such as floods or earthquakes mean money must be spent on recovery.
  - Many countries in Africa are landlocked (surrounded by other countries) so access to ports and trade routes is difficult.
  - Access to valuable natural resources may be difficult or expensive.

> **Key Point**
>
> These factors must be considered and understood if countries are to be helped to develop effectively.

Dry conditions and natural disasters can hinder development opportunities

Where are the Developed and Developing Countries?

- The North/South divide refers to the fact that most of the countries in the Northern Hemisphere are developed, whereas many countries in the Southern Hemisphere are less developed.
- The **Brandt Line** is an imaginary line that divides the developed north from the less developed south.
- In some respects, the Brandt Line is misleading and outdated because many countries below the line are NICs (for example, India and China).

North/South divide

Brandt Line

HIC
LIC

> **Quick Test**
>
> 1. What type of indicators help us to understand how developed a country is?
> 2. Give one example of a social indicator.
> 3. Why is there a trade deficit in many developing countries?
> 4. Explain the concept of the Brandt Line.

> **Key Words**
>
> indicators
> trade deficit
> debt
> Brandt Line

Development 2

Quick Recall Quiz

You must be able to:

- Understand the importance of composite development indicators
- Recall the aims of the UN's development goals
- Consider the problems of aid
- Define and understand the importance of sustainable development
- Understand what is meant by 'fair trade' and its benefits.

Composite Indicators

- Development is measured by combining a variety of indicators that examine the economic, social and cultural characteristics of a country. These are known as 'composite indicators'.
- The **Human Development Index (HDI)** measures life expectancy, knowledge (adult literacy and education) and standard of living (GDP per capita).
- The HDI is a more meaningful measure of a country's level of development than looking at indicators separately because it takes into account both economic and social measures. Individual measures can be misleading.
- India, for example, has a GDP that is almost twice as large as that of Australia, but in 2022 India had a low HDI figure of 0.647 (131st highest in the world) compared with Australia's 0.944 (7th highest in the world).

> **Key Point**
>
> The closer the Human Development Index figure is to 1, the more developed the country; Norway, for example, scores 0.957.

The United Nations Development Goals

- The United Nations (UN) is an organisation formed in 1945 that works for international peace and security. Most of the world's countries are members.
- In 2000 the UN agreed to eight goals aimed at promoting development globally.
- These goals focussed on meeting basic human rights that are needed for a higher quality of life. They included:
  - universal education
  - child health
  - reduced child mortality
  - an end to poverty and hunger.
- Countries were scored annually on progress with a target date to meet the goals by 2015. Progress was uneven, and in 2016 the UN replaced the Millennium Development Goals with the Sustainable Development Goals.
- The Sustainable Development Goals are a set of 17 goals with 169 targets that all UN members have agreed to work towards achieving by the year 2030. These goals include:
  - the ending of poverty
  - the ending of hunger and achieving food security

European headquarters of the UN, Geneva

> **Key Point**
>
> Basic human rights are the rights of each person on the planet to health, education, shelter and security.

- ensuring inclusive education for all
- taking action to tackle climate change.

Problems of Aid

- Aid can be provided by a country, a group of countries or charity groups, like Save the Children and Oxfam.
- But aid is often given with conditions attached. These conditions often benefit the **donor** more than the **recipient**:
  - Aid may be given in the form of large projects that are run by the HIC, meaning profits may be greater for the donor.
  - Large projects may be undertaken without proper consideration of their effects on the environment.
  - Corrupt LIC governments may prevent the aid from going where it is needed most.
  - Aid may lead to **dependency** on the HIC.
  - Aid may be in the form of loans that result in LICs struggling even more than before as their debt repayments increase.

Sustainable Development

- If development is to be successful and sustainable then money must form just one part of the development process.
- Economic sustainability, social sustainability and environmental sustainability must all be considered.
- **Sustainable development** is development that meets the needs of the present without compromising the ability of future generations to meet their own needs.

Fair Trade

- **Fair trade** is where producers receive a guaranteed fair price for the things they make and grow. A fair price is one that covers costs of production and enables people to have a reasonable standard of living. It also puts money into community projects like improving access to clean water.
- Fair trade ensures that trade is beneficial to the LIC and not controlled unfairly by the HICs it trades with.
- The Fairtrade Foundation was developed in the UK to ensure this happens.

Key Point

Fair trade contributes to sustainable development by assisting social, environmental and economic progress.

Key Words

Human Development Index (HDI)
donor
recipient
dependency
sustainable development
fair trade

Quick Test

1. What are composite indicators?
2. Why can GDP be a misleading measure of development?
3. Give two problems of aid.
4. Define the term 'sustainable development'.

Economic Activity 1

You must be able to:

- Classify economic activities into different groups
- Understand what sort of jobs people do in different countries
- Understand where people get their food from.

Quick Recall Quiz

Economic Activity

- Economic activity is defined as human actions that deal with the production, distribution and consumption of goods and services.
- Individuals and companies carry out economic activities to earn money:
    - Individuals use the money to live – to pay for goods and services.
    - In the case of a company, the aim is to make a profit.
- There are four main kinds of economic activity:
    - primary
    - secondary
    - tertiary
    - quaternary.

> **Key Point**
>
> There are four main kinds of economic activity – primary, secondary, tertiary and quaternary.

Primary Activities	**Primary activities** involve natural resources, such as minerals, timber, fossil fuels and food. The products can be grown or dug out of the ground and then sold. Some are processed into other things (oil is used to produce fertiliser and other chemicals) but many can be used as they are (bananas).	
Secondary Activities	**Secondary activities** involve making or **manufacturing** things from natural resources. This usually happens in factories. Examples include making bread from wheat and other ingredients, making paper from trees, building a car using many different materials (metal, plastics, rubber and glass).	
Tertiary Activities	**Tertiary activities** involve providing a **service** for other people or organisations. Examples include teaching, nursing, police services, estate agents and all types of shop work.	
Quaternary Activities	**Quaternary activities** involve collecting, processing, analysing and providing information. Examples include scientific research and business consultancy services. The quaternary sector is sometimes included with the tertiary sector as they both relate to providing a service.	

- In the UK and other HICs:
  - most people (70–80%) work in the tertiary and quaternary sectors
  - many secondary activities employ few people, as machines and robots do much of the work
  - only a small percentage of people work in primary activities such as farming and mining.
- In the LICs, there is a great deal of variation. For example:
  - in some LICs, such as Nigeria, the majority of people still work on the land growing their own food
  - in other LICs, such as Pakistan, a growing number now live in cities and work in factories.

Farming and Food Production

- In LICs people still work on the land to provide their own food. If they have a small surplus, they may sell it at a local market. The money can be used to buy other goods and services. Such farms are usually small and inefficient.
- Many LICs have now developed large, modern farms that provide food not for local people but for HICs, such as the UK and USA.
- In the UK we buy food from around the world so that all types of food are available all year round.
- Although we can grow all of these in the UK, examples of imported food include strawberries, asparagus, sweetcorn, green beans and apples.
- Farms in LICs also grow non-food products including:
  - cotton
  - oilseed
  - flowers
  - medicinal herbs.
- Many of these non-food items are exported to industrial countries where they are processed into useful products such as cotton for clothing, or oilseed for biofuels.
- In the UK we grow about 60% of the food we need and the rest is imported. We couldn't grow all our own food as things such as oranges, sweet potatoes and rice need a much hotter climate to grow.
- Most UK farms are very modern and highly mechanised. They use large amounts of chemicals to make the crops grow and to kill off bugs and weeds. Some farms are organic, which means they use no chemicals.
- **Arable** farms grow the plants that we eat (potatoes, carrots, wheat, etc.) and **pastoral** farms rear the animals that provide us with eggs, milk and meat.

A farm worker in a LIC

Key Point

In the UK, we grow about 60% of the food we eat. The rest is imported from around the world.

Mechanised farming in the UK

Quick Test

1. Why do people carry out economic activities?
2. What kind of economic activity is nursing?
3. What is a food surplus?
4. Why do farmers grow cotton?

Key Words

primary activity
secondary activity
manufacturing
tertiary activity
service
quaternary activity
arable
pastoral

Economic Activity 2

You must be able to:

- Explain the different things that are needed for a factory
- Outline where different products are made
- Explain what kind of work is done in the tertiary sector.

Quick Recall Quiz

Manufacturing Industry

- Humans have always made the items they need from natural resources. Over the last 200 years most manufacturing has been done in factories and workshops.
- It is cheaper and more efficient to make lots of the same items in a factory so we now have factories that specialise in making particular goods such as computers, cars and smartphones.
- Factories need land to build on, natural resources to make their products, energy to power the factory, **labour** (workers), and good transport links to import raw materials and move products to market.
- In the past, factories needed lots of labour but today much of the work is **mechanised**, i.e. done by machines. In car factories, specialised robots do a lot of the repetitive or dangerous jobs.

Inside a modern factory

Manufacturing Industry in NICs

- Although the UK still has a manufacturing industry – we make cars, clothes, chemicals and food products for example – much manufacturing is now done in LICs and NICs (**newly industrialising countries**).
- In countries such as China, Brazil and Mexico, workers are paid much less so factories have lower labour costs. Land may also be cheaper and environmental laws not so strict about pollution and waste products.
- Many **textiles** (clothing) were made in the UK in the past but today the majority of the world's textiles come from Asia.
- Many UK companies with well-known labels, such as New Look, GAP, Monsoon, River Island, Primark, TK Maxx, Topshop, Burton and Miss Selfridge import their clothes from Asia.
- There are often complaints of factory workers being badly treated with very low wages and long hours of work without a break. Such factories are called 'sweatshops'.
- Another important industry is the **high-tech** factories that make computers, tablets, smartphones and TVs. Japan and the USA were famous in the past for making many of these products but many Japanese and American companies have now moved their factories to Taiwan, Singapore, Malaysia and China.

> ### Key Point
>
> A large amount of manufacturing now takes place where labour costs are lower.

> ### Key Point
>
> India, Bangladesh and China have large numbers of textile factories employing millions of people, mainly women.

Textile workers in Asia

- Some NICs have now become world leaders in high-tech products. The best example of this is in South Korea, where in 2012, Samsung Electronics became the world's largest mobile phone maker, and had about 30% market share in 2019.

Providing a Service

- In the HICs, the majority of jobs are now in the tertiary sector – providing a service for other people and organisations.
- The sort of work carried out in the service industries varies from low-skilled and low-paid jobs (shop assistants, office cleaners, care workers, security guards, etc.) through to highly skilled professionals who require degree qualifications and years of training (lawyers, doctors, dentists, vets, etc.).
- One of the most important service sectors in the UK is the **retail** or shopping sector, which provides jobs for over three million people.
- There are many different kinds of work in retail from sales assistant, through customer services and marketing, to finance and management.
- People working in retail may be located in town centres but also increasingly in edge-of-town shopping centres such as Bluewater in Kent, Meadowhall in Sheffield, the Metrocentre in Newcastle and the Trafford Centre in Manchester.
- Many high streets now have identical sets of shops with well-known names as smaller family businesses have increasingly closed down.
- Supermarkets have taken over from many small butchers, bakers and fruit and vegetable shops.

A modern, edge-of-town shopping complex

Quick Test

1. Why do factories need good transport links?
2. What is an NIC?
3. Name one high-tech product.
4. Name two of the UK's major edge-of-town shopping centres.

Key Words

labour
mechanised
newly industrialising
   countries (NICs)
textiles
high-tech
retail

Natural Resources 1

You must be able to:

- Explain what natural resources are and give examples
- Understand the difference between renewable and non-renewable resources
- Show your knowledge of different kinds of trees and what they are used for.

What are Natural Resources?

- **Natural resources** are resources found in nature. Humans need these natural resources in order to survive and to enjoy a good quality of life.
- Some natural resources are **renewable** and, used carefully, will go on being available for many years into the future. For example, plants and animals will reproduce themselves so long as we do not deplete their numbers too drastically.
- Unfortunately, humans often don't use resources carefully, which means that there is a danger they could disappear.
- For example, in the North Sea, overfishing has reduced fish numbers to such an extent that there are not enough left to replenish the stocks. Fishing boats now have to sail further away from the UK to find fish.
- A **sustainable** use of resources means using them carefully so there are enough for future generations to use.
- An example of sustainable use would be to plant two young trees every time we cut down a mature tree to use the timber. This will ensure a plentiful supply of trees for future generations.
- Some natural resources are **non-renewable**. They have taken millions of years to be created and once used up, there will be no more.
- Examples of non-renewable resources are fossil fuels (coal, oil and natural gas) and mineral resources such as iron ore and copper.
- To make non-renewable resources last longer, we have to either use smaller quantities or, where possible, try to **recycle** them. Many metals can be recycled and used again.

> **Key Point**
>
> Humans need to use natural resources carefully (sustainably) so that they are still around for future generations.

A recycling logo

Forestry Resources

- Wood has always been an important natural resource. People use it for building their homes, for fuel and for paper making.
- Coniferous trees are softwood trees:
  - They grow in areas with cool climates such as Northern Europe, Canada and northern Russia.
  - They are quick growing (25–30 years to reach full size) and ideal for building and for paper making.

- Millions of softwood trees are planted and cut down each year. Coniferous trees are not in short supply as they grow very quickly.
- Deciduous trees, such as oaks, are hardwood trees:
  - They grow in both temperate and tropical areas such as the UK and Brazil.
  - They are slow growing (80–120 years to reach full size) and the timber is prized for high value products such as furniture and ornaments.
- The tropical rainforests contain hardwood trees such as mahogany and teak.
- To find the rare and valuable trees, whole areas of rainforest are cleared. This destroys the natural environment where other plants, animals and insects live.
- Some people believe that the rainforests should be preserved but the local people need work and the timber that is exported earns money for the government to pay for schools, roads and hospitals.
- A single teak tree may be worth over £10 000.

Coniferous tree

Deciduous tree

Tropical rainforest

Quick Test

1. How are natural resources created?
2. Why do we need natural resources?
3. Name one natural resource.
4. Will all natural resources forever be available for humans to use?

Key Words

natural resources
renewable
sustainable
non-renewable
recycle

Natural Resources 2

Quick Recall Quiz

You must be able to:

- Understand why there are now declining numbers of fish in the seas and oceans
- Name the different fossil fuels and describe where they come from
- Understand what different fossil fuels are used for.

Resources from the Sea

- The seas, oceans and lakes around the world have always been used by humans to find food and other resources.
- The main source of food from the sea is fish. Humans also collect shellfish, prawns, seaweed, coral and salt from the sea.
- A large percentage of the fish living in the seas and oceans has now disappeared due to **overfishing**. It is getting harder to find fish in large numbers in areas near to where people live.
- A lot of the fish that we now eat comes from **fish farms**. The fish are reared in indoor tanks and then put into shallow lakes or offshore in cages where they are fed artificially with pellets of fish food. Salmon and trout are good examples of fish reared in this way.
- Although a few small, local fishing boats still exist, most sea fishing is done by huge **factory ships** and trawlers. These catch fish indiscriminately in huge nets, whether useful or not. Useful fish are processed and frozen at sea in the factory ships – anything unwanted is thrown back into the sea dead or dying.

Fresh fish produce

Key Point
Many natural supplies of fish have now disappeared due to overfishing and we depend increasingly on fish farms for our food.

Fish farm

Energy Resources

- **Fossil fuels** have provided humans with energy for the last 150 years.
- Coal has been mined for much longer than this but became important during the Industrial Revolution when it was used in a variety of ways:
  - in furnaces to smelt iron and later steel
  - in coal fires to heat homes
  - in steam engines that powered factory machines and railway engines.
- Coal is no longer a major source of energy in the UK. Less than 3% of the electricity used in the UK is generated using coal. The use of coal has been reduced because of the levels of pollution and greenhouse gases produced by burning coal.

- The most important fossil fuel is now natural gas. About 36% of our electricity comes from burning natural gas in **power stations**. Natural gas is also used in homes for heating and cooking.
- We import an increasing amount of natural gas. Most of our gas imports arrive by pipeline from Norway and the Netherlands and by tanker from Qatar in the Middle East.
- Oil or petroleum is only rarely used in power stations but it is one of our most important natural resources. Oil is piped to refineries where it is converted into many different products such as petrol, diesel, engine oil, plastics, fertilisers, pesticides and a variety of important drugs such as aspirin.
- Both oil and natural gas are found under the North Sea so they are collected by drilling rigs that are connected by pipeline to the coast. Both of these natural resources are slowly running out.
- With domestic resources of fossil fuels increasingly depleted or economically unviable, the UK is producing more and more of its energy from renewable sources such as wind, solar and hydroelectric power. This is also contributing to efforts to combat climate change by reducing carbon dioxide emissions.

Power station

> ## Key Point
>
> Fossil fuels are a non-renewable resource but we currently depend on them to produce electricity and many of our everyday essential items.

North Sea oil rig

> ## Quick Test
>
> 1. What is the main natural resource that we get from the sea?
> 2. What fossil fuel was used to power machines 100 years ago?
> 3. What is made in a power station?
> 4. Where does the UK get its gas from?

> ## Key Words
>
> **overfishing**
> **fish farm**
> **factory ship**
> **fossil fuel**
> **power station**

Ordnance Survey Maps 1

You must be able to:

- Identify direction
- Calculate distance using scales
- Locate places using four-figure grid references.

Direction

- Direction is given on a map using the points of the **compass**.
- The **cardinal points** of a compass going clockwise are north, east, south and west. You can remember their order using the mnemonic 'Naughty Elephants Squirt Water'.
- North is always at the top of an **Ordnance Survey (OS)** map.
- On OS maps light blue **grid lines** run from north to south and from east to west.

Scale

- Scale is indicated on an OS map using a ratio, a **scale line** and the size of the grid squares.
- The most common scales on OS maps are 1:50 000 and 1:25 000.
- 1:50 000 means that the map is 50 000 times smaller than the places that it shows, so that 2 cm on the map is equal to 1 km in reality. The grid squares on the map are 2 cm × 2 cm.
- 1:25 000 means that the map is 25 000 times smaller than the places that it shows, so that 4 cm on the map is equal to 1 km in reality. The grid squares on the map are 4 cm × 4 cm.

Measuring Distance

- There are a number of ways to measure distance on a map: one of the easiest is to count the number of grid squares from one point to another. This is a quick way of finding the distance between places to the nearest kilometre.
- Another method is to use a piece of paper and lay it against the scale line printed on the map.

  1 Place the paper between the two places you want to measure.

  2 Mark the two places on the paper.

  3 Place the paper along the scale line for the map, with the mark indicating the first place at the zero on the scale line.

  4 Write down the distance on the scale line indicated by your mark for the second place.

Points of the compass

Four-Figure Grid References

- Four-figure **grid references** are used to locate an area of 1 km² on an OS map. This is the area of one grid square.
- To find the four-figure grid reference of a square on an OS map:
  1. Go along the bottom of the map until you reach the line at the left-hand side of the square.
  2. Write down the two digits of this line.
  3. Go up the side of the map until you reach the line at the bottom of the square.
  4. Write down the two digits of this line.
  5. You should now have a four-figure grid reference.

Key Point

Remember to use the digits at the bottom of the map first, followed by the digits at the side of the map. Say to yourself, 'along the corridor and up the stairs'.

Uffington Village: Grid Reference 3089

Key Words

compass
cardinal points
Ordnance Survey (OS)
grid lines
scale line
grid references

Quick Test

1. Which direction is always at the top of an OS map?
2. How large are the grid squares on a 1:50000 OS map?
3. What size area does a four-figure grid reference locate?

Ordnance Survey Maps 2

You must be able to:

- Locate places using six-figure grid references
- Understand the relief (shape) of the land using contour lines
- Use a key to understand map symbols effectively.

Six-Figure Grid References

- Six-figure grid references are used to locate an area of 100 m × 100 m on an OS map.
- To find the six-figure grid reference of an area on an OS map:
  1. Go along the bottom of the map until you reach the line at the left-hand side of the grid square that the area is in.
  2. Write down the two digits of this line.
  3. Divide the bottom of the grid square into 10, with 5 being in the middle of the square.
  4. Count along the bottom of the grid square until you reach the area, then write down the digit you have got to, after the two digits you have just written.
  5. Go up the side of the map until you reach the line at the bottom of the grid square that the area is in.
  6. Write down the two digits of this line.
  7. Divide the side of the grid square into 10, with 5 being in the middle of the square.
  8. Count up the side of the grid square until you reach the area, then write down the digit you have got to, after the two digits you have just written.
  9. You should now have a six-figure grid reference.

> **Key Point**
>
> Remember that the half-way point from one side of a grid square to the other is 5, therefore the grid reference for the middle of a grid square will always be xx5xx5.

Land relief on an OS map

contour line

Relief

- **Relief** is the height and shape of land.
- Relief is shown on an OS map using **contour lines** and **spot heights**.
- Contour lines are thin brown lines that join up places of equal height above sea level; they are usually drawn in 10-metre intervals.
- Spot heights are points on a map with a precise measurement of the height above sea level in metres printed on the map.
- **Triangulation points** are used by surveyors to measure the height of the land; they are indicated on an OS map with a blue triangle and a height above sea level in metres printed next to it.

> **Key Point**
>
> The closer contour lines are together, the steeper the slope will be.

Map Symbols

- Map symbols can be divided into different types to make them easier to understand. If you are unsure what a map symbol means always look it up in the key (a key is shown below).
- Footpaths are marked using solid or dashed red lines on a 1:50 000 map and green lines on a 1:25 000 map.
- Forests and woods are shown by blocks of green containing symbols representing the different types of tree: deciduous, coniferous or mixed.
- Buildings are drawn as pink rectangles and important buildings are edged in a thick black line.
- Some buildings are drawn as symbols such as churches, lighthouses and windmills.
- OS maps also use abbreviations for some important buildings including:
  - PH = public house (pub)
  - Sch = school
- Tourist information is shown on OS maps using blue symbols.

Revise

Key Point

1:25 000 maps are large-scale maps, which means that they show more detail than 1:50 000 maps. For example, 1:25 000 maps show field boundaries (hedges and fences) as thin black lines, which makes it much easier to navigate on a walk, whereas 1:50 000 maps do not.

Key Point

There is a wider range of tourist information on 1:25 000 scale maps in comparison to 1:50 000 maps.

OS map key

ROADS AND PATHS
Not necessarily rights of way

Junction number
Service area 1 Elevated
S
M1 Dual carriageway
A 493
B 4518

- Motorway (dual carriageway)
- Main road
- Secondary road

RAILWAYS

- Track multiple or single
- Track under construction
- Siding
- Tunnel
- Light rapid transit system, narrow gauge or tramway

- Bridges / Footbridge
- Level crossing LC
- Viaduct
- Station, (a) principal
- Light rapid transit system station

ANTIQUITIES

- + Site of monument
- Castle Non-Roman

TOURIST INFORMATION

- ▲ Youth hostel

ABBREVIATIONS

- P Post office
- PC Public convenience (in rural areas)
- PH Public house
- TH Town Hall, Guildhall or equivalent

Quick Test

1. By how much do you have to divide the side of a grid square when you are working out a six-figure grid reference?
2. What is the usual interval between contour lines?
3. What colour are motorways on an OS map?
4. What does PH stand for on an OS map?

Key Words

relief
contour lines
spot heights
triangulation points

Review Questions

Rivers and Coasts

1 What are the three main stages along a river's course? [3]

2 a) What are the four main processes of erosion? [4]

b) Name one landform resulting from erosion. [1]

c) Name one landform resulting from deposition. [1]

3 Say whether each cause of flooding is a human cause or a physical cause by drawing lines to connect the boxes.

| Saturated soil |
| Urbanisation |
| Impermeable rock |
| Heavy rain |
| Deforestation |

| Human cause |
| Physical cause |

[5]

4 What features of rock will affect rates of weathering and erosion along coastlines? [2]

5 What is the difference between constructive waves and destructive waves? [2]

6 Draw lines to match the type of rock to its example.

| Soft rock |
| Hard rock |

| Chalk |
| Sandstone |
| Granite |

[3]

7 What process transports material along the coastline? [1]

8 Suggest two groups of people who might disagree about how the coast should be managed. Suggest how the groups might disagree. [3]

Landscapes

1　**a)** Define the term 'exploit'. [2]

　　b) Give two examples of humans exploiting natural landscapes. [2]

2　Why is overpopulation a problem for natural landscapes? [3]

3　**a)** What is the name of the gas that is released when rainforests are burned?
Tick (✓) the correct option.

Oxygen ☐

Methane ☐

Nitrogen ☐

Carbon dioxide ☐ [1]

　　b) Why does this contribute to global warming? [1]

4　**a)** Which two characteristics of climate change can lead to desertification?
Tick (✓) the correct options.

Increased wet periods ☐

Increased dry periods ☐

Lower temperatures ☐

Less rainfall ☐ [2]

　　b) Give two characteristics of soil that has suffered desertification. [2]

5　**a)** Explain how deforestation leads to soil erosion. [2]

　　b) Why does planting trees prevent soil erosion? [2]

6　**a)** Why are rainforests being removed? [2]

　　b) Define the term 'indigenous'. [2]

　　c) Why are indigenous people so important for the future of rainforests? [3]

Population

1. The graph shows how the world population is growing.

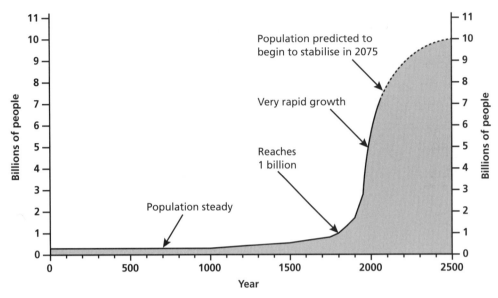

a) Why is the world population growing very quickly at the moment? [2]

b) Why is it likely, eventually, to level out at around 10 billion people? [3]

2. Name two areas of the world which have a sparse population and explain why so few people live there. [4]

3. Which area has the higher population density? Give data to support your answer.

   A London

   B Highlands of Scotland [2]

4. Why might a civil war lead to many refugees arriving in a neighbouring country? [2]

5. What is happening to birth rates in most LICs? Tick (✓) the correct option.

   Rising ☐

   Falling ☐

   Staying the same ☐ [1]

6. Why do many HICs have high death rates? [2]

7. Why might migrants from Eastern Europe move to countries elsewhere in the European Union? [2]

Urbanisation

1 **a)** What do HIC and LIC stand for? [2]

    b) Which group of countries is currently experiencing rapid urbanisation? [1]

2 **a)** Why did people start to move away from cities in the UK? [3]

    b) Name two processes that illustrate this movement away from city centres. [2]

3 **a)** Which of the following are characteristics of urban decline? Tick (✓) the correct options.

    Full employment ☐

    Crime ☐

    High quality housing ☐

    Abandoned shops ☐

    Derelict factories ☐ [3]

    b) What is urban regeneration? Give an example. [3]

4 The photo shows a megacity.

    a) What is a 'megacity'? [1]

    b) Where are megacities growing most rapidly? [1]

5 What three aspects must be considered when managing cities? [3]

6 How can homes be energy efficient? [4]

Development

1 a) What does development measure?   [1]

   b) What types of indicator can be used to measure development?   [2]

   c) Give three examples of social indicators.   [3]

   d) Give two examples of economic indicators.   [2]

2 Which types of industry dominate in LICs? Give examples.   [4]

3 Explain how physical factors can influence the level of development in LICs.   [4]

4 The image shows the Brandt Line. Explain why the Brandt Line is no longer a
   meaningful description of the location of developed and developing countries.   [2]

5 Why is the Human Development Index a useful way of understanding development?   [4]

6 Use the following key words to complete the paragraph about the problems of giving aid.

   environment   **recipient**   **attached**   **corrupt**   **dependency**   **donor**

   Aid is often given with conditions _____, which often benefit the _____

   more than the _____.

   Large aid projects don't always consider the fragile _____ in which they're built.

   _____ LIC governments may prevent the aid from going where it is needed most. Aid may

   lead to aid _____ on the HIC.   [6]

7 a) Explain the concept of sustainable development.   [5]

   b) How does fair trade contribute to sustainable development?   [5]

Economic Activity

1 Why do companies carry out economic activities? [1]

2 Draw lines between the boxes to match each of these workers to the sector they are classified as.

Market researcher		Primary
Teacher		Secondary
Coal miner		Tertiary
Baker		Quaternary	[4]

3 a) Give two examples of natural resources produced by primary workers. [2]

   b) Give two examples of jobs in the tertiary sector. [2]

   c) Calculate the missing percentages at A, B and C below.

	Primary	Secondary	Tertiary & Quaternary
Nigeria	A	10%	20%
China	38%	B	34%
United Kingdom	2%	18%	C	[3]

4 a) Name two farm products that can be grown in the UK but are often imported. [2]

   b) How much of the food eaten in the UK is grown by UK farmers? [1]

5 Fill in the missing words to complete the following sentence.

Factories need land to build on, _____ _____ to make their products and

_____ to power the factory. [3]

6 a) Name two countries where most clothing is now manufactured. [2]

   b) What is a 'sweatshop' factory? [2]

7 Which of these jobs would be low skilled and low paid? Tick (✓) the correct options.

Office cleaner ☐   Dentist ☐

Security guard ☐   Teacher ☐ [2]

Practice Questions

Natural Resources

1. Where are natural resources found? [1]

2. If we make use of our natural resources in a sustainable way, why is that a good thing? [2]

3. What is the problem with non-renewable natural resources? [1]

4. Give two reasons why wood is an important natural resource. [2]

5. a) How long does it take for a coniferous tree to reach full size? Tick (✓) the correct option.

    25–30 years ☐

    55–60 years ☐

    75–80 years ☐ [1]

    b) Why is there no shortage of coniferous trees? [2]

6. a) Name one type of hardwood tree that grows in the rainforest. [1]

    b) Why is it important that some of the rainforest is preserved? [2]

7. a) What is a fish farm? [2]

    b) What happens in a factory ship? [2]

8. Other than in power stations, where and for what purposes is natural gas used? [2]

Ordnance Survey Maps

1 Study this extract of the Landranger 1:50 000 Ordnance Survey
Map around Newquay in Cornwall.

one grid square is 1 km

a) Give the four-figure references for: **i)** the village of Cubert **ii)** Penhale Point   [2]

b) Name the villages in the following grid squares: **i)** 8256   **ii)** 7658   [2]

c) What is the straight-line distance between the car park at Fistral Beach and the
hospital in Newquay?   [1]

Geographic Information Systems 1

Quick Recall Quiz

You must be able to:

- Understand what a Geographic Information System (GIS) does
- Explain how a GIS can be used in real life
- Describe the different sorts of data used in a GIS.

GIS Overview

- A **Geographic Information System (GIS)** brings together hardware, software and data. A GIS can be used to capture, manage, analyse and display all forms of information that is georeferenced.
- At a simple level, a GIS can be used to view data on maps. The data can be changed, analysed and viewed in different ways to help gain an understanding of geographical patterns and relationships.
- In order to use a GIS, you need:
  - a computer or tablet
  - GIS software to organise the data
  - digital data, including map data and other sorts of data such as census information.
- Geographic Information Systems have been used in the real world for many years now. Examples include the following:
  - The police service uses GIS to plot crime patterns, enabling them to focus on crime prevention in key areas.
  - The ambulance service uses GIS to keep track of where each ambulance is positioned and which one can respond most quickly to an emergency call.
  - Water, gas and electricity companies use GIS to map the positions of underground pipes and cables so that they know where it is safe to dig. They also record the condition of the pipes and cables.
  - Supermarkets use GIS to plan their deliveries. All supermarket goods come from giant warehouses and hundreds of lorries transport the goods across the UK each day to the different supermarkets.

> **Key Point**
>
> A Geographic Information System (GIS) is a combination of computer hardware, GIS software and digital data.

GIS being used to survey an area

How does a GIS work?

- A GIS consists of **layers of information** (like sheets of paper) stacked on top of each other. The GIS software has a key that allows you to switch layers on or off. Layers can also be made transparent so that you can see the layer beneath.

GIS layers

People

Roads

Relief

Land use

The real world

- The base layer is usually a digital map but it could be a photo or satellite image.
- The features on the digital map are divided into four types:
  1. **Points** are symbols that represent a feature at a particular point location, e.g. a trig point that shows the top of a mountain.
  2. **Lines** are symbols that show things like roads and rivers.
  3. **Polygons** cover an area and may be a regular shape such as a square to represent a building or an irregular shape to represent something like a lake.
  4. Text is used for the names of places, or landscape features, e.g. Mount Snowdon, River Thames, Heathrow Airport.
- Digital maps will show both natural and manufactured features. The relief or shape of the land is shown by numbered contour lines. This data can be used to show the land as a 3D image with hills and valleys.
- In the UK, digital map data is created and published by the Ordnance Survey (OS). It produces paper maps as well as digital data for computers, tablets, smartphones and satellite navigation systems (sat navs).

Key Point

GIS software shows digital data in layers that can be switched on or off to help understand the geographical patterns and relationships.

Key Words

Geographic Information System (GIS)
layer of information
point
line
polygon

Quick Test

1. What do the letters GIS stand for?
2. What do the police use a GIS for?
3. What might a line on a digital map show?
4. Who produces digital maps in the UK?

Geographic Information Systems 2

Quick Recall Quiz

You must be able to:

- Outline what kinds of online GIS are available for free
- Understand how you can use these geotechnologies in different ways
- Use and add data to Google Earth.

Geotechnologies

- It is now possible to use many different kinds of **geotechnologies** (geographical technologies) for free online. Some local councils, for example, put all their digital data into online GIS systems, providing local maps showing leisure facilities, waste disposal facilities, parks and open spaces, local footpaths and shopping centres.

- Online GIS provided by commercial organisations and local authorities allow you to view different kinds of data but you cannot enter your own data or alter the data shown on the maps. An exception to this is Wikimapia, a publicly created map that allows users to add features to help build up the information presented.

> **Key Point**
>
> Many GIS are now available for free online so that the public can access map data.

Google Earth

- A good way of doing some GIS work for free is to use Google Earth (GE). Google Earth is a **virtual globe** with maps and a variety of GIS data that can be added as layers and which also allows you to add your own data.

- In Google Earth you can zoom through different scales from the initial global view, through national to local scales. In this way, you can see where places are located and how they relate to other places. This helps to develop your spatial understanding in geography.

Google Earth is a free online GIS

GIS enable you to view the world in different ways

- Google Earth has built-in layers for borders, roads, weather, land use and much more. You can choose which layers you want to view in the Layers Panel.
- One of the most exciting geographical features is that you can view 'live' layers in which the data is regularly updated. In this way you can see changing cloud cover or where the latest earthquake has happened.
- Most of the data shown in Google Earth comes from high resolution **satellite imagery** and as you zoom in, you can see settlements, roads and land use. At a local level, satellite images are replaced by **aerial photos** taken from aircraft. These allow you to see much finer detail such as your house and garden!
- Google Earth has a timeline feature that allows you to view a sequence of superimposed images showing how an area has changed over time. In this way, you can see how a city such as New Delhi in India has grown in size or how large areas of the tropical rainforest in Brazil have been lost.
- Google Earth allows you to plot your own data and save the maps. You can add:
  - placemarks
  - polygons
  - paths
  - images
  - text boxes
  - videos.
- You can also do 'tours' in Google Earth that allow you to fly automatically from one part of the world to another. You can even fly under the sea and view the ocean floor!

Key Point

A satellite is a spacecraft launched into orbit around the Earth (or another planet or body in the solar system) in order to collect information or for communication.

GIS offers all sorts of exciting opportunities

Key Point

Google Earth is a powerful and free online GIS system that can be downloaded on to computers, tablets and smartphones.

Quick Test

1. What is geotechnology?
2. What do the letters GE stand for?
3. What can you do in the Layers Panel in Google Earth?
4. What is a satellite?

Key Words

geotechnology
virtual globe
satellite imagery
aerial photo

Fieldwork 1

Quick Recall Quiz

You must be able to:

- Explain what is meant by fieldwork
- Understand how to make fieldwork successful
- Collect different kinds of data safely and accurately.

Fieldwork Overview

- **Fieldwork**, sometimes called **Learning Outside the Classroom (LOtC)**, is a vital part of work in geography. It involves working outside the classroom in order to observe phenomena or to collect data about the real world.
- Fieldwork or LOtC can happen in the school grounds, in the local neighbourhood, a different part of the UK or most adventurous of all – overseas fieldwork in another country.
- The fieldwork process usually involves work outside and then work back in the classroom:
  - collating data
  - displaying data
  - analysing data
  - drawing conclusions.
- Most fieldwork is linked to **enquiry-based learning** which means using a question as a starting point and then trying to find evidence to answer that question.
- For successful fieldwork it is important to have:
  - good planning
  - proper equipment, footwear and clothing
  - a positive attitude to the work
  - an awareness of health and safety at all times
  - co-operation: much fieldwork involves group work.

Data Collection

- Data is the information we collect when working outside the classroom. Accuracy of data collection is very important. You need to learn how to use tools and fieldwork equipment.
- There are many different ways to collect data. These include using our eyes and recording what we see on paper. This could be a description of an actual object (a tall, white chalk cliff) or our **perception** (I think this area looks dangerous/untidy/unfriendly). Perception is about how we feel.
- We can take photos or sound recordings to record what we see and hear. It is helpful if these are **georeferenced**. This means recording the location using co-ordinates (latitude/longitude or a grid reference). Some equipment does this automatically.

> **Key Point**
>
> Fieldwork, or Learning Outside the Classroom, is a very important part of work in Geography. It allows you to experience the real world.

Collecting data

> **Key Point**
>
> A lot of data is collected systematically, i.e. at regular intervals (e.g. every 5 minutes or every 10 metres).

Collecting data

- In different types of fieldwork, we might measure different things:
  - Urban study (e.g. types of housing, amount of litter, noise levels).
  - Shopping study (e.g. types of shops, number of pedestrians, size of shop frontage).
  - River study (e.g. width of stream, stream velocity, slope angle).
  - Beach study (e.g. width of beach, pebble size, types of waves).
  - Microclimate study (e.g. temperature, wind speed, sunshine/shade).
  - Soil study (e.g. soil depth, soil texture, soil moisture).
- Data collection can involve using special equipment such as a wind vane (to measure wind direction), a flow meter (to measure velocity or speed of river flow) and a quadrat (a one-metre square metal grid).
- Data collection can involve making judgements. To help quantify the judgement, we may use something like a **bi-polar scale**:

Key Point

There are many different ways to collect data. It is important to be accurate and learn how to use tools and equipment.

| Clean | +5 | +4 | +3 | +2 | +1 | 0 | −1 | −2 | −3 | −4 | −5 | Dirty |

- Questionnaires are a very useful way to collect information from people. They can be anonymous (no names) but should include some personal details such as age group (0–16, 17–35, 36–50, over 50) and gender (male/female/non-binary). This allows us to see if different groups of people give different answers.
- Questionnaires can have open questions that give space for people to give an opinion or they can have closed questions that give people several things to choose from and then ask them to tick one box.

Do you think the supermarket should be built on this site?

_____

_____

Which is your favourite take-away food?

a) Burger King [   ]   **b)** McDonalds [   ]

Collecting data

Open question

Closed question

Key Words

fieldwork
Learning Outside the Classroom (LOtC)
enquiry-based learning
perception
georeference
bi-polar scale

Quick Test

1. What do the letters LOtC mean?
2. Why is co-operation important for successful fieldwork?
3. What is a grid reference an example of?
4. What is a wind vane used for?

Fieldwork 2

You must be able to:

- Present data on maps and as graphs
- Understand which method of data presentation is most appropriate.

Data Presentation

- **Data** collected during fieldwork can be presented in many different ways. It is helpful to organise the data so that it can be analysed and conclusions can be drawn.
- Presenting data on maps is an important geographical skill. Sometimes we want to show change over time. This can be done by using a **historical map** from the OS (Ordnance Survey) and then drawing our own map to show what something is like now. An example of this would be to show the location of new housing estates in a town that is growing in size.
- A choropleth map is a useful way to show how something varies across a map. It could show, for example, how the pedestrian density varies in different parts of a town:

> **Key Point**
>
> There are many different ways to present fieldwork data. It is important to choose the most appropriate method.

Pedestrian density map
(number of people per hour)

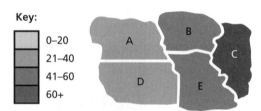

Key:
- 0–20
- 21–40
- 41–60
- 60+

- If you have taken photos or made fieldwork sketches, these can be annotated with labels to present information about your topic:

Meander

Trees prevent flooding

Gentle gradient

Sedimentary rock

High banks formed by erosion

Annotated fieldwork photo

- Much of the data that you want to present can be turned into different types of graphs. It is important to choose the right sort of graph:

Line graph

- If you are showing changes over time, then you need to draw a **line graph**. A good example would be to show how temperature changes over time at a particular place. If you wanted to compare two places, you could plot two lines on the same axes.

Bar chart

- If you are showing different amounts of something in different categories, then a **bar chart** would be a good choice. As an example, you could show how the number of houses of each type (detached, semi-detached, terraced, bungalow) varies in a town.

- A pie chart is a useful method if you want to use percentages rather than **raw data** (original data). So for example, you could work out the percentage of people travelling to work by car/bus/walking/cycling and show this as a pie chart.
- **Pictograms** or picture graphs are an interesting way to present data. You need to decide on a symbol or picture to represent the amount, e.g. one stick person = 10 people. You can then, for example, draw stick people to represent the number of people visiting different types of shop. It is a good idea to choose a symbol which can clearly be interpreted if you need to represent a fraction of the number.

> **Key Point**
>
> Presenting data helps us to understand the information that we have collected whilst working outside the classroom and to draw conclusions.

Pie chart

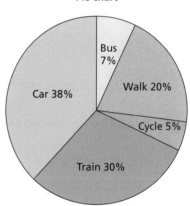

Bus 7%, Walk 20%, Cycle 5%, Train 30%, Car 38%

Quick Test

1. What do the letters OS mean?
2. What is a fieldwork sketch?
3. If 25 people walk to work and 75 people catch the bus, what percentage use public transport?
4. What is a pictogram?

> **Key Words**
>
> data
> historical map
> line graph
> bar chart
> raw data
> pictogram

Practice Questions

Geographic Information Systems

1 What are the three things that you need for a Geographic Information System (GIS)? [3]

2 What, at a simple level, is a GIS used for? [1]

3 **a)** Why does the police service plot crime data on a GIS? [2]

    b) Name one other organisation that uses GIS. [1]

4 Why might you make a GIS layer transparent? [1]

5 **a)** What sort of information is shown as a point on a GIS layer? [1]

    b) What sort of information is shown as a line on a GIS layer? [1]

6 Read the following sentences and tick (✓) the ones that are true.

You cannot add data on most online GIS. ☐

You can add data on most online GIS. ☐

You can change data on most online GIS. ☐

You cannot change data on most online GIS. ☐ [2]

7. What sort of information might you find on an online local council GIS?
Give two examples. [2]

8 **a)** What is Google Earth? [2]

    b) How can you learn about scale in Google Earth? [4]

9 **a)** What information can you see on a satellite image in Google Earth?
Give two examples. [2]

    b) Complete the following sentence by filling in the missing words.

    As you zoom in from the global view in Google Earth, the satellite images are

    replaced by .... [1]

Fieldwork

1 **a)** What is another name for fieldwork? [1]

b) Draw lines to match each part of fieldwork with where it is normally carried out.

| Displaying data |
| Analysing data |
| Taking photos |
| Conducting surveys |
| Drawing conclusions |

| Outdoors |
| In the classroom |

[5]

c) Why is the correct equipment, footwear and clothing important for successful fieldwork? [2]

2 Why must you be accurate when collecting data? [2]

3 Suggest two things that might be measured on a shopping study. [2]

4 What is a flow meter used for? [2]

5 Is the following question an open question or a closed question?

How many times a week do you walk to school?

1 ☐ 2 ☐ 3 ☐ 4 ☐ 5 ☐

[1]

6 Why might you use a historical map when presenting your fieldwork data? [2]

7 **a)** When would you use a bar chart to present fieldwork data? [2]

b) Why might you use a pictogram to show fieldwork data? [1]

Review Questions

Development

1 a) What term is used to describe developing countries?   [1]

   b) Give an example of a developing country.   [1]

2 What do social indicators measure?   [2]

3 Define the term 'life expectancy'.   [2]

4 Give an example of a secondary industry.   [1]

5 What does NIC stand for? Tick (✓) the correct option.

   Newly independent country   ☐

   Northern industrialised country   ☐

   Newly industrialising country   ☐

   Newly independent company   ☐   [1]

6 Why are many LICs in debt?   [3]

7 Which of the following were Millennium Development Goals?
   Tick (✓) the correct options.

   Child health   ☐

   Reduced child mortality ☐

   Improved environment   ☐

   An end to poverty   ☐

   Greener transport   ☐

   Universal education   ☐   [4]

8 Define the term 'sustainable development'.   [3]

Economic Activity

1 Economic activities can be divided into four groups. Name the groups. [4]

2 What does the word 'manufacture' mean? [1]

3 a) What do farmers in LICs do with their surplus food? [2]

   b) Where does the food grown on large farms in LICs usually end up? Give an example. [2]

4 a) Why do some farmers use large amounts of chemicals? [2]

   b) What is the difference between an arable farm and a pastoral farm? [2]

5 Underline the correct word in the following sentence:

   If work in a factory is mechanised, it is done by **hand/machines**. [1]

6 a) Name two products still made in factories in the UK. [2]

   b) Which of the following products might be made in a high-tech factory?
   Tick (✓) the correct options.

   A toy ☐

   A book ☐

   A smartphone ☐

   A pizza ☐

   A TV ☐ [2]

7 Which company is the world's largest mobile phone maker (by number of handsets sold)?
Tick (✓) the correct option.

   Apple ☐

   Nokia ☐

   Blackberry ☐

   Samsung ☐ [1]

Review Questions

Natural Resources

1. What is special about renewable natural resources? [2]

2. What happens when we recycle natural resources? Give an example. [2]

3. The photo shows coniferous trees.

   a) Are coniferous trees hardwood or softwood trees? [1]

   b) How long does it take for a deciduous tree to reach full size?
      Tick (✓) the correct option.

   10 years ☐   50 years ☐   Over 100 years ☐   [1]

   c) Why is it important that some of the rainforest trees are chopped down? [2]

4. a) Name two natural resources that humans collect from the sea. [2]

   b) What effect does overfishing have on the natural resources in the sea? [2]

5. a) How much of our electricity in the UK comes from burning coal?
      Tick (✓) the correct option.

   Less than 3% ☐   23% ☐   33% ☐   53% ☐   [1]

   b) Why does burning coal cause problems for the environment? [2]

6. a) How important a fuel is oil in our power stations? [1]

   b) Name two products made from oil that are used by farmers. [2]

Ordnance Survey Maps

1 Study this extract of the Landranger 1 : 50 000 Ordnance Survey Map around Newquay in Cornwall.

a) Why do six-figure grid references give a more accurate location than four-figure grid references?

[2]

b) Give six-figure grid references for:

   i) the public house south of Rejarrah Farm on the A3075   [2]

   ii) the T-junction in Goonhavern of the B3285 with the A3075.   [2]

c) What is found at the following grid references?   [2]

   i) 786577   [2]

   ii) 785542   [2]

   iii) 811617   [2]

d) Locate square 8355 and give the six-figure reference for:

   i) the big building in the north-west corner of the square   [2]

   ii) the golf course   [2]

   iii) the deciduous forest in the south-west corner of the square.   [2]

Geographic Information Systems

1 How does a GIS help the ambulance service?   [1]

2 **a)** In a GIS, what does a layer show? Give an example.   [2]

   b) Why might you switch layers on or off?   [2]

   c) What is usually used as the base layer in a GIS? Tick (✓) the correct option.

     A quadrat   ☐

     A graph   ☐

     A map   ☐   [1]

   d) Name one other type of information that could be used as a base layer.   [1]

3 What sort of information is shown as a polygon on a GIS layer?   [1]

4 Why is text needed on a GIS layer?   [1]

5 What does a Google Earth tour do?   [2]

Fieldwork

1 **a)** Where might you carry out local fieldwork? Tick (✓) the correct options.

France ☐

In another country ☐

In the school grounds ☐

In the local neighbourhood ☐ [2]

b) Which part of the fieldwork process is carried out 'in the field'? [1]

2 Why is health and safety important for successful fieldwork? [1]

3 What is a georeferenced photo? [2]

4 Describe two things that might be measured on a beach study. [2]

5 **a)** What is an anonymous questionnaire? [1]

b) Give an example of an open question that could be used on a questionnaire. [2]

6 What is the name given to this type of map? [1]

Increase in tonnes per annum
- 0–20
- 21–40
- 41–60
- 61–80
- 81–100
- 101–120
- >120

7 Look at the data in the table.

People Visiting Different Kinds of Shops			
Food	Clothes shop	Phone shop	Sports shop
120	46	24	10

a) Convert this raw data into percentages. [4]

b) Draw a pie chart to display the data. [4]

Mixed Test-Style Questions

1 **a)** Explain why individuals and companies carry out economic activities.

....

....

....

....

2 marks

b) Describe the kind of work done by people working in primary activities.

....

....

....

3 marks

c) State whether each of the following sentences is **true** or **false**.

i) In HICs, 70–80% of people work in the tertiary
and quaternary sectors. ....

ii) In HICs, a large percentage of people work in the primary sector. ....

iii) In LICs such as Nigeria, most people work in the tertiary
and quaternary sectors. ....

3 marks

2 Name the countries from their outlines. (*Not to scale*).

a) **b)** **c)**

a) ....

b) ....

c) ....

3 marks

3 **a)** List three similarities between South Korea in 1953 and Kenya today.

....

....

....

3 marks

b) Describe what it is like to live in South Korea today.

....

....

....

3 marks

4 **a)** Name three processes of erosion that take place in rivers.

....

....

....

3 marks

b) The photos show landforms found at different stages of rivers.

Underneath each one, write **upper**, **middle** or **lower** to show where each is found.

i)

Meander

ii)

Waterfall

iii)

Floodplain

....

3 marks

TOTAL

23

Mixed Test-Style Questions

5   Explain, with examples, the difference between renewable and non-renewable resources.

5 marks

6   Describe the arguments for and against cutting timber from tropical rainforests.

4 marks

7   a) Name the three main rivers in the Middle East.

3 marks

   b) Explain why major cities in the Middle East are often located close to rivers.

2 marks

   c) Which other natural resource has influenced economic development in the Middle East and why hasn't every country in the Middle East benefited from this?

2 marks

8 **a)** Match the letter of each picture with the named rocks below.

A   B   C

Granite ....

Sandstone ....

Chalk ....

3 marks

b) Granite is an igneous rock. Describe the characteristics of igneous rocks.

....

....

....

3 marks

9 Define the term 'urbanisation'.

....

....

2 marks

10 Some development indicators are measured 'per capita'. What does 'per capita' mean?

....

....

1 mark

11 Draw a graph with labelled axes to show how world population has grown over the last 100 years and add some annotations.

6 marks

TOTAL

31

12 Explain, with examples, why few people choose to live in difficult environments.

....

....

....

....

....

4 marks

13 **a)** Name a **cold** desert and a **hot** desert.

Cold desert   ....

Hot desert   ....

2 marks

b) Describe the similarities and differences between hot deserts and cold deserts.

....

....

....

....

4 marks

14 Which of the following are examples of fragile landscapes? Tick (✓) the correct options.

Tropical rainforests   ☐   Deciduous woodlands   ☐

Deserts   ☐   Savannah grasslands   ☐

2 marks

15 **a)** Explain how mountains are formed when tectonic plates move.

....

....

....

....

3 marks

b) Look at the diagram. What type of plate boundary is shown?

☐

1 mark

16 **a)** Study the photograph below. Name the type of weathering that is shown.

☐

1 mark

b) Draw lines to match each statement to the type of weathering it describes.

Happens in cold, mountainous areas	Biological weathering
Often occurs in deserts due to the temperature change	Freeze-thaw weathering
Takes place when weak acid in rainwater dissolves rocks	Chemical weathering
Occurs when plants and animals break down rocks	Onion-skin weathering

☐

4 marks

TOTAL

☐

21

17 **a)** Explain how a glacier can shape the landscape.

....

....

....

....

4 marks

b) Name one glacial landform that results from deposition.

....

1 mark

18 Why have many city centres experienced decline over time?

....

....

....

....

3 marks

19 Describe the difference between each type of precipitation.

....

....

....

....

4 marks

20 How would we measure the two different wind elements at a weather station?

....

....

....

....

4 marks

21 Study the graph below showing the effect of angle of slope and land use on soil erosion.

a) Which land use creates the most soil erosion?

....

b) Explain why less soil erosion takes place where the land use is forest.

....

....

....

....

4 marks

c) Which of the following are ways that farmers can reduce the amount of soil erosion from their fields?

Tick (✓) the correct options.

Cattle grazing

Contour ploughing

Building terraced fields

Building dry-stone walls

Planting trees

3 marks

TOTAL

24

Mixed Test-Style Questions

22 Describe three ways that Kenya is connected to the UK.

....

....

....

....

....

....

3 marks

23 a) Why are fossils an important part of the Geological Timescale?

....

....

....

....

3 marks

b) Place the following creatures into the flowchart to show the order in which they appeared on Earth.

Humans   Fish   Dinosaurs   Birds

Earliest ☐ → ☐ → ☐ → ☐ **Latest**

4 marks

24 What happens to the Earth during a period of glaciation?

....

....

....

....

....

4 marks

25 The photograph shows a favela in Sao Paulo, Brazil. Explain why shanty towns might develop in LICs.

....

....

....

....

☐

5 marks

26 a) Explain why you might collect data when doing fieldwork.

....

....

....

....

☐

4 marks

b) What sort of annotations might you add to a fieldwork photo taken in the high street of a town centre?

....

....

....

....

☐

4 marks

TOTAL

☐

27

27 What equipment might you need for a microclimate study in the school grounds? What would you record?

....

....

....

....

....

....

⬜ 4 marks

28 **a)** Which of the following are examples of hard engineering? Tick (✓) the correct options.

Building dams ⬜   Restricting building on floodplains ⬜

Giving flood warnings ⬜   Creating reservoirs ⬜   ⬜ 2 marks

b) Using examples, outline the advantages and disadvantages of hard and soft engineering on the coast.

....

....

....

....

....

⬜ 4 marks

29 **a)** Using an example, explain why a GIS is a useful tool.

....

....

....

....

....

⬜ 4 marks

b) Why doesn't it matter how many layers you have in a GIS?

....

....

....

....

2 marks

c) Explain the difference between a line and a point in a GIS.

....

....

....

....

4 marks

30 Imagine you are a farmer who lives in a post-glaciated landscape. Write a letter to the council explaining your concerns about the increasing tourist numbers.

Dear Sir/Madam

5 marks

TOTAL

25

Mixed Test-Style Questions

31 Explain, with examples, why many of the goods we buy are made in LICs or NICs.

2 marks

32 Why in general are earthquakes more dangerous than volcanoes?

3 marks

33 What are the similarities and differences between tropical climates and desert climates?

3 marks

TOTAL

8

Answers

Key Concepts from Key Stage 2

1. a) Equator – C [1]; Tropic of Capricorn – D [1];
        Tropic of Cancer – B [1]; Greenwich Meridian – A [1]
    b) i) Brazil – Yellow [1]   ii) Argentina – Turquoise [1]
        iii) Italy – Red [1]   iv) USA – Orange [1]
        v) Sweden – Turquoise [1]
2. a) i) Richter scale [1]   ii) Epicentre [1]
        iii) Extinct [1]
    b) i) A – Source [1]; B – Tributary [1]; C – Confluence [1];
        D – Mouth [1]; E – Watershed [1]
        ii) evaporation [1]; condensation [1]; precipitation [1];
        run-off [1]; throughflow [1]
3. a) Primary activity – Farmer [1]; Secondary activity – Metal
        worker [1]; Tertiary activity – Dentist [1]; Quaternary activity
        – Programmer [1]
    b) i) cities [1]   ii) hamlet [1]   iii) conurbation [1]

Page 7 Quick Test
1. Taiga
2. Permafrost
3. The Volga
4. 5.5 million

Page 9 Quick Test
1. Any three: rice; tea; wheat; cotton; peanuts; tobacco
2. 400 million; current limit is three children per couple
3. Yangtze; 6300 km
4. The Communist Party

Page 11 Quick Test
1. Alpine tundra
2. July to September
3. The Indus
4. 1947

Page 13 Quick Test
1. 2.3 million km^2
2. It is the largest sand desert in the world
3. Arab
4. Islam, Christianity (or other suitable answer)

Page 15 Quick Test
1. 582 650 km^2
2. Between January and March
3. Nairobi

Page 17 Quick Test
1. 30%
2. Temperate monsoon
3. 51.3 million

Page 19 Quick Test
1. 4.6 billion years old
2. Charles Darwin
3. North Wales and north-west Scotland
4. 160 million years

Page 21 Quick Test
1. There was no atmosphere
2. As an adaptation to extreme cold
3. Factories and transport
4. A few centimetres per year

Page 23 Quick Test
1. The core
2. Plates

3. Destructive
4. Conservative

Page 25 Quick Test
1. Very common – thousands may occur every day
2. The focus is where an earthquake starts
3. Due to the ground cracking and gas pipes breaking
4. The molten rock that comes out of a volcano

Page 26: Location Knowledge – Russia, China, India and the Middle East

1. a) It has fertile soil [1] called chernozem [1].
    b) 38°C [1] 250 mm [1]
2. a) i) Moscow [1]
        ii) 12.5 million [1]
    b) Death rates [1] are rising [1] and people are having fewer
        children [1] due to economic uncertainty [1].
3. People can own and run their own businesses [1]. The
    government has encouraged international trade [1].
4. It has hot wet summers [1], cold dry winters [1] and fertile land
    from river sediments [1].
5. a) A small percentage increase will have a dramatic effect on
        India's already large population [1]. Increasing wealth may
        encourage people to have more children (although often
        family size decreases when a country becomes richer) [1].
        Some religions do not condone contraception [1].
    b) India has such a large population that its GDP per capita is
        small [1]. Inequality means that the majority of the wealth
        in concentrated into the hands of a minority [1].
6. He campaigned for independence for India [1] from the British
    Empire [1] and was the first prime minister [1] of an independent
    India [1].
7. a) 6.5 million km^2 [1]
    b) Europe [1]; Africa [1]; Asia [1]
8. It connects the Mediterranean Sea to the Red Sea [1], allowing
    sea transport between Europe and Asia [1] without having to go
    around Africa [1].

Page 27: Africa and Asia Compared – Kenya and South Korea
1. a) Western Kenya [1]
    b) It is formed by the African Plate [1] stretching and slowly
        tearing apart [1], so the land is sinking [1].
2. Coffee [1]; Tea [1]; Flowers [1]
3. Kenya is a poor country [1]. It does not have the resources to
    cope with rapid population growth [1] and struggles to provide
    housing, jobs, education and healthcare [1].
4. a) 2.5 million [1]; safari [1]; Mombasa [1]
    b) Tourism provides jobs for 800 000 Kenyans [1]. It is a source
        of overseas money for the country [1], providing 25% of
        Kenya's export earnings [1].
5. A large South Korean company [1] that produces a wide range of
    goods and services [1]
6. a) Built new roads [1]; took control of factories [1]; concentrated
        on manufacturing industry [1]; built new schools [1]
    b) It grew from $872 [1] to $7455 [1]
7. South Korea's longest river is the Nakdong River [1]. A free trade
    agreement exists between the EU and South Korea [1].
8. a) 2012 [1]
    b) 19 people were killed [1]; 1.9 million homes lost power [1];
        $374.3 million worth of damage [1]

Page 28: Geological Timescale
1. a) The Geological Timescale shows the history of the Earth
        related to different rock types [1] and the fossils associated
        with them [1].

b) 1 billion years after the Earth was first formed **[1]**

c) A fossil is the remains of a plant or animal **[1]** trapped in the rocks **[1]**.

2. Dinosaurs **[1]**
3. The group of apes that humans belong to **[1]**
4. It didn't rain when the Earth was first formed as there was no atmosphere **[1]**.
5. a) During the last glaciation, humans moved south **[1]** to where it was warmer **[1]**.

   b) During a glaciation, the sea level falls **[1]** as the water is trapped on land as ice **[1]**.
6. Greenhouse gases trap heat in the atmosphere **[1]**. The climate becomes warmer **[1]**.

Page 29: Plate Tectonics

1. a) A – Core **[1]**; B – Mantle **[1]**; C – Crust **[1]**

   b) Because it is relatively thin when compared to the overall size of the Earth **[1]**

   c) 5000°C

   d) It causes the rocks in the mantle to become soft **[1]** and they slowly flow **[1]**.
2. Pangaea **[1]**
3. a) An earthquake is a violent shaking of the ground where tectonic plates are moving alongside each other **[1]**.

   b) Most damage is caused at the epicentre **[1]** as this is the point on the surface directly above the focus of the earthquake **[1]**.
4. Waves up to 30 m (100 ft) high **[1]** killed large numbers of people living along the coast **[1]**.
5. International aid is help or money given by countries to help people who have suffered a natural disaster such as an earthquake **[1]**, e.g. medical supplies or rescue teams **[1]**.
6. Volcanoes in Hawaii are low and wide **[1]**. Land near volcanoes is fertile **[1]**.

Page 31 Quick Test

1. Porous
2. Erosion; transportation; deposition; lithification
3. Lava
4. Igneous

Page 33 Quick Test

1. Rainfall, temperature and atmospheric gases
2. It freezes and expands
3. Oxygen and water
4. The tree puts roots through joints and cracks in the rocks, causing them to split open.

Page 35 Quick Test

1. The breakdown of rocks by the action of the weather, plants and animals.
2. It has to fluctuate (rise and fall) above and below zero degrees.
3. Hot during the day and cold at night.

Page 37 Quick Test

1. Humus
2. Nutrients, minerals and humus
3. 20–30 metres

Page 39 Quick Test

1. Weather is the daily changes in the atmospheric conditions.
2. Any three: rainfall; sleet; snow; hail
3. An anemometer measures wind speed.

Page 41 Quick Test

1. Temperature and rainfall
2. Between the Tropics of Cancer and Capricorn
3. A desert climate
4. The height of the land

Page 43 Quick Test

1. Plucking and abrasion
2. Firn forms when accumulated snow begins to become compacted and dense.
3. Bowl shaped/armchair shaped/steep back wall and lip at the front
4. The main valley glacier cuts off smaller glaciers, leaving the smaller valleys hanging above the main valley.

Page 45 Quick Test

1. Egg or teardrop shaped with a tapered end downstream.
2. They are transported over long distances from their origins.
3. Any two: footpath erosion; noise/water pollution from speedboats; dog walkers disturb sheep; traffic jams

Page 46: Location Knowledge – Russia, China, India and the Middle East

1. –50°C **[1]**
2. a) Materials that are found in the natural environment **[1]** that are useful to people **[1]**.

   b) Information technology **[1]**; nanotechnology **[1]**; space industry **[1]**
3. Beijing **[1]**; 21.5 million **[1]**
4. a) 12th May **[1]** 2008 **[1]**

   b) 8 **[1]**

   c) 87 000 **[1]**
5. 700 000 km² **[1]**
6. Hindu **[1]**
7. Any four: motor vehicles **[1]**; shipbuilding **[1]**; chemicals **[1]**; telecommunications **[1]**; computers **[1]**; software development **[1]**; pharmaceuticals **[1]**; textiles **[1]**; agriculture **[1]**; mining **[1]**
8. a) Arabian **[1]**; Sahara **[1]**

   b) 650 000 km² **[1]**; 250 m **[1]**
9. Qatar **[1]**; Bahrain **[1]**; Kuwait **[1]**; Oman **[1]**

Page 47: Africa and Asia Compared – Kenya and South Korea

1. Two times larger
2. 1390 mm **[1]**, similar to the UK **[1]**
3. A type of tropical rainforest found in upland areas **[1]** where there is very high humidity. **[1]**
4. Mt Hallasan **[1]**; 1950 metres **[1]**
5. Any three: oak; birch; spruce; yew **[3]**
6. 83.3 years **[1]**
7. a) 1945 **[1]**; Japan **[1]**

   b) 3 million **[1]**

Page 48: Geological Timescale

1. Sedimentary rocks **[1]**
2. a) Precambrian rocks **[1]**

   b) North Wales and north-west Scotland **[1]**
3. The creatures that survive are those that are best adapted **[1]** to their environment **[1]**.
4. The dinosaurs became extinct when an asteroid **[1]** struck the Earth **[1]**.
5. a) Africa **[1]**

   b) Modern-day humans **[1]**

   c) The brains of modern-day humans are much larger than those of their ancestors **[1]**.
6. If we are in an interglacial period **[1]** and an ice age returns **[1]**
7. a) The chalk in south-east England formed from sediments deposited in a warm, tropical sea **[1]** when the UK was located much further south than now **[1]**.

   b) The UK had a desert climate **[1]** many millions of years ago **[1]**.

Page 49: Plate Tectonics

1. a) Where two plates meet **[1]**

   b) Examples: Alps in Europe; Himalayas in Asia; Andes in South America; Rocky Mountains in North America **[1]**

c) When two plates move apart at a constructive plate boundary, molten magma [1] from the mantle [1] fills the gap.
2. The UK and the USA are on different plates [1] and the two plates are moving very slowly apart [1].
3. a) A tsunami is a large wave [1] caused by underwater earthquakes [1] which shake the seabed [1].
   b) Any two examples: damage to buildings, roads, railways, bridges, underground pipes and cables [2].
   c) Many people may die after an earthquake due to injuries [1] or a lack of food and water [1].
4. A volcano formed where hot magma [1] breaks through a weak area in the Earth's crust [1].
5. a) Two plates meet here [1] and molten rock escapes to form volcanoes [1].
   b) The soil is very fertile [1] and good for growing crops [1].

Pages 50–53 **Practice Questions**

Page 50: Rocks and Geology
1. a) Igneous rocks are formed when magma cools [1] and solidifies [1].
   b) If magma cools slowly, the rock will have large crystals [2]; if magma cools quickly, the rock will have small crystals [2].
2. a) 28% [1]
   b) limestone = marble [1]; shale = slate [1]
3. Sedimentary rocks [1] are most likely because the remains of plants and animals become trapped between layers of sediment on the ocean floor [1].
4. You can clearly see the layers in the rock [1], which show that it was formed from layers of sediment over millions of years [1].

Page 51: Weathering and Soil
1. a) Cold mountainous environments [1]
   b) A – 2 [1]
      B – 3 [1]
      C – 1 [1]
2. Plant roots [1] and animal burrows [1] can break up and destroy rock.
3. a) climate = high temperatures increase the rate of soil formation [1]; organisms = insects, worms and plants [1]; parent material = the type of rock that the soil has weathered from [1]; relief = the shape of the land [1]
   b) Time [1]
4. 75 billion tonnes [1]
5. Latosol [1]

Page 52: Weather and Climate
1. Humidity [1]; wind [1]
2. Minimum temperature = Lowest temperature recorded each day [1]; Humidity = Amount of moisture in the air [1]; Precipitation = Amount of moisture that reaches the ground [1]
3. Hail is a pellet of ice falling from a cloud [1].
4. It will increase the air pressure (high pressure) [1].
5. Examples: farmer, fisher, pilot, construction worker, driver, etc. plus a logical reason for the choice, e.g. a farmer would use the weather forecast to help decide when to sow seeds (Any example with explanation for [2]).
6. When air is warmed by the Sun, it rises (low pressure) [1].
7. A = (Average) temperature [1]; B = (Average) rainfall [1]
8. Either side of the Equator between the Tropic of Cancer [1] and the Tropic of Capricorn [1].
9. The Gulf Stream is a warm ocean current [1] that flows from the Gulf of Mexico [1] towards the UK [1].

Page 53: Glaciation
1. a) A large moving body of ice [1] that flows slowly down a valley due to the force of gravity [1].
   b) The last glacial period [1]
   c) When more snow falls than can melt, the snow builds up: accumulation [1]; over time, the weight of the snow causes it to become compacted and dense [1]; at this stage it is called firn [1]; the weight of the ice mass causes it to slide and advance downhill [1] due to gravity [1].

2. Freeze-thaw [1]; plucking [1]; abrasion [1]
3. A = lateral [1]; B = medial [1]; C = terminal [1]
4. a) an obstruction [1] b) deposited [1] c) streamlines [1]
   d) advancing [1]
5. Footpaths may become overused [1], meaning vegetation is destroyed and land is eroded [1]. Speedboats [1] may lead to noise and water pollution [1]. Tourists may not be aware of farming practices [1] and their dogs could disturb livestock [1]. (Three impacts clearly explained for [6].)

Pages 55–69 **Revise Questions**

Page 55 Quick Test
1. Attrition; corrasion/abrasion; hydraulic action; solution
2. The act of depositing a sediment
3. Deposition

Page 57 Quick Test
1. Waves and weather
2. The wind
3. Longshore drift
4. Tourists/environmentalists

Page 59 Quick Test
1. Growing populations need land and resources.
2. Trees absorb carbon dioxide from the atmosphere.
3. Between forest and desert environmental regions.
4. The process by which land becomes infertile and unproductive desert.

Page 61 Quick Test
1. They find food, clothing and building materials from the forest.
2. They know how to live a sustainable existence and can inform management strategies based on this knowledge.
3. Replacing trees that have been cut down.
4. Circles of stones placed on the ground to prevent water run-off.

Page 63 Quick Test
1. 85 million people
2. There will not be enough resources for all the extra people.
3. These areas do not have the resources that people need.
4. Western Europe has the resources that people need to survive and have a good quality of life – water, flat land, fertile soil, minerals.

Page 65 Quick Test
1. Emigrants leave a country and immigrants arrive in a country.
2. Refugees need food and shelter after being forced to flee their homes.
3. UK: 11.3 (BR) – 9.4 (DR) = 1.9
   India 17.1 (BR) – 7.3 (DR) = 9.8
4. People eat lots of 'junk food' and do not exercise enough.

Page 67 Quick Test
1. The process by which the proportion of people living in urban areas grows.
2. People are pushed from rural areas by lack of jobs/good healthcare/education and pulled to the cities by the attraction of opportunities for work/education, resulting in the growth of towns and cities and the decline of rural areas.
3. People move out from city centres to avoid pollution and overcrowding.
4. Following economic/social and environmental decline as people and jobs moved away from cities.

Page 69 Quick Test
1. In HICs urbanisation occurred at a steady rate; in LICs it has happened more rapidly.
2. Makeshift housing on unwanted land around the city
3. When local people are involved in the planning/management process
4. Social, economic and environmental factors

Page 70: Rocks and Geology

1. Rock that can absorb water [1]
2. a) i) Older rocks [1] and the remains of living organisms [1]
      ii) Any three from: chalk [1]; limestone [1]; sandstone [1]; shale [1]; clay [1]; coal [1]; conglomerate [1]; breccia [1]
   b) i) Heating [1]; applying (extreme) pressure [1]
      ii) Any three from: marble [1]; slate [1]; schist [1]; gneiss [1]
3. Intrusive rocks are igneous rocks that have formed from magma that has solidified inside the Earth [1] whereas extrusive rocks are igneous rocks that have formed from magma that has solidified on the surface of the Earth [1].
4. A = Eroded particles transported by rivers to the sea [1]; B = Particles sink to the bottom of the sea [1]; C = Particles build up in layers [1]; D = Over millions of years new rock forms on the seabed [1]
5. Igneous rocks are formed from molten rock beneath the Earth's surface [1], known as magma [1]. This includes rocks made from lava from volcanic eruptions [1] or rocks made from solidified magma underground [1].

Page 71: Weathering and Soil

1. Calcium carbonate [1]; carbonic acid [1]
2. 1 – Water gets into cracks in rocks [1]; 2 – water freezes and expands [1]; 3 – rocks split and break up [1]
3. Changes in temperature cause the surface of the rock to expand and contract [1] because it is exposed to the direct heat of the Sun/cooling effect of the night [1]; this creates stress between the surface of the rock and its core [1] because they are expanding and contracting at different rates [1].
4. Weathering is the breakdown of rocks in situ (in one place) by the action of plants, animals and the weather [1]; erosion is the removal of weathered material by the action of wind or water [1].
5. a) Ploughing horizontally across slopes [1] in order to minimise soil erosion [1].
   b) Because it can take hundreds of years for soil to form [1]
   c) Any three from: type of soil [1]; angle of slope [1]; strength of the wind [1]; water flowing over the surface [1]; vegetation cover [1]
6. 1–2 m deep [1]; thick topsoil (20 cm) [1]; took 10 000 years to form [1]
7. a) 45% [1]
   b) 10 000 years [1]

Page 72: Weather and Climate

1. Hail [1]; snow [1]
2. a) The wind may bring warm or cold air depending on where it comes from [1].
   b) High wind speeds can cause damage to trees and buildings [1].
3. South-east England [1]
4. On a foggy day humidity will be high [1]
5. A weather forecast for the next 24 hours [1] as it is difficult to predict the weather a long way into the future [1].
6. The UK has average temperatures of around 5°C in winter [1] and around 17°C in summer [1] so the difference is about 12°C [1].
7. a) Polar, tundra, temperate, desert, tropical. (One mark per correct answer up to a maximum of 4.) [4]
   b) The temperature would be hot all year round [1] with a high total rainfall [1].
8. The Sun strikes the Earth at a low angle near the poles [1] and is reflected back into space [1].

Page 73: Glaciation

1. Snow builds up [1] when more snow falls than can melt [1]
2. When melting [1] is greater than accumulation [1]
3. Ribbon lake [1]
4. In a corrie [1] after the glacier has melted [1]

5. A = pyramidal peak [1]; B = U-shaped valley [1]; C = hanging valley [1]
6. The material deposited [1] on a valley floor after a glacier melts [1]
7. Look out of place [1] because they usually have a completely different rock type [1] from those in the locations where they are dropped.
8. A beautiful/scenic area/landscape [1] that attracts large numbers of tourists [1] during seasonal months [1]
9. a) Any three from: farmers [1]; environmentalists [1]; tourists [1]; local councils [1]; residents [1]
   b) They may forget to keep dogs on leads [1], which means livestock may be harmed [1]; may overuse footpaths [1] and cause soil erosion and the destruction of vegetation [1].
   c) They can educate the tourists about the landscape [1]; provide information [1] to inform tourists on which paths to use to avoid overuse [1] or how to behave around farmland [1].

Page 74: Rivers and Coasts

1. Erosion [1]; transportation [1]; deposition [1]
2. Rocks carried within the water [1] erode the river bed and banks [1].
3. Any one from: waterfall; V-shaped valley; rapids; gorge [1]
4. Meander [1]; A = erosion [1]; B = deposition [1]
5. A river will flood when water reaches the channel faster than it can be carried downstream [1]. Overland flow can lead to flooding as this is the fastest route to the channel [1].
6. Wind blows over the surface of the sea [1]; oscillations are caused by friction between wind and sea [1]; wave energy is transferred forward in the direction of the prevailing wind [1]; wave height increases due to friction between sea and seabed [1]; top of wave moves faster than bottom [1]
7. A = wave-cut notch [1]; B = wave-cut platform [1]
8. Advantages: immediate/effective coastal protection [1]; groynes prevent longshore drift and create wide beaches [1] Disadvantages: can be expensive to maintain [1]; can be an eyesore [1]; can limit access to the beach [1]; might destroy natural habitats [1] (One advantage and one disadvantage for [2])

Page 75: Landscapes

1. A growing population [1] means that towns and cities are increasing in size [1].
2. Any three from: removing trees and vegetation [1] to make space for farming and cities [1]; digging mines and quarries [1] for natural resources [1]; controlling rivers [1] for electricity [1]
3. Example: Amazon rainforest [1]; 390 billion trees [1]; trees act as a carbon sink for CO_2 emissions [1]
4. a) They find food, clothing and building materials in the forest [1] so do not require manufactured goods/fuel [1]; move their villages regularly [1] to allow the landscape to recover and grow back [1]; live a sustainable existence [1] because they use the land without destroying the environment [1]. (Points must be explained for [4].)
   b) Populations are decreasing because many have died from introduced diseases such as measles [1]; been forced into cities [1]; had their environment destroyed by deforestation [1].
   c) By working with indigenous people, we can learn important information about rainforests — their ecology [1], medicinal plants [1], food and other products [1]; people can teach [1] valuable lessons about managing rainforests sustainably [1].
5. Conservation of savannah landscapes [1] can protect them from desertification because areas are protected from overgrazing/over-cultivation [1]. Trees are planted [1] to protect soils and prevent soil erosion [1]. Terracing [1] means soil is not washed down the slope when it rains [1].

Page 76: Population

1. a) Any answer from 7.7 to 7.8 billion people [1]
    b) In the past population growth was low [1] but now it is very fast [1].
    c) Over 10 billion [1]
2. In a sparse population, there are few people [1] whereas in a dense population, there are many people [1].
3. The area has many resources, such as oil, that attract industry and people [1].
4. High population density examples: Bangladesh, South Korea [1]; low population density examples: Peru, Russia [1]
5. An illegal immigrant does not have permission to enter a country and may be asked to leave [1] whereas a refugee has lost their home and has special permission to seek help in another country [1].
6. If the birth rate is higher than the death rate, then there will be a natural increase in the population [1].
7. A family planning campaign aims to reduce [1] the number of babies being born [1].
8. Too many older people who require lots of expensive care [1]; too few people of working age so not enough people to do the jobs [1]

Page 77: Urbanisation

1. a) The process by which the proportion of people living in urban areas grows [1]; more people live and work in towns and cities than remain in the countryside [1].
    b) Rural-to-urban migration [1] means people migrate from the countryside to the cities [1]; natural increase [1] means more births than deaths [1].
    c) More machines like tractors means fewer people are needed to work [1]; this means fewer jobs in rural areas [1]; people move to cities to find employment [1].
2. Suburbanisation is the growth of urban areas around a city centre [1]; counterurbanisation is the growth of smaller villages and towns [1] beyond the main urban area [1].
3. a) People moving away from cities [1]; industry moving away from cities [1]; means that inner cities are declining economically [1], socially and environmentally [1].
    b) Example: The London Docklands Development Corporation [1] was set up in 1981 to attract new businesses; money and people back to the area [1].
4. Unlike the steady growth of HIC cities over 200 years [1], LIC cities have grown rapidly in just 60 years [1].
5. a) Corrugated iron roofs [1]; no electricity [1]; no waste disposal [1]; lack of roads [1]
    b) Local people [1] are granted ownership of their land [1] and provided with training [1] and tools to improve the homes themselves [1].
6. Six appropriate characteristics identified:
    Walking and cycling is safe – pedestrianised streets [1]
    Recycling bins [1]
    Open green spaces [1]
    Traffic calming in roads [1]
    Bus and bike lanes [1]
    Street lighting makes cities safer [1]
    Energy efficient homes (e.g. with solar panels/well insulated) [1]

Page 79 Quick Test

1. Varying economic, social, technological and cultural levels of development across the world
2. Examples include: life expectancy; infant mortality rates; literacy rates
3. They spend more on their imports than they make on their exports.
4. An imaginary line on the world map dividing the wealthy north from the poor south

Page 81 Quick Test

1. Development measures that combine a variety of indicators to examine the economic, social and cultural characteristics of a country.

2. GDP can be high, but social development may still be low.
3. Is often tied to conditions unfavourable to the LIC; can cause LICs to become dependent on aid and can lead to huge debts.
4. Development that meets the needs of the present generation without compromising the ability of future generations to meet their own needs.

Page 83 Quick Test

1. People carry out economic activities to earn money.
2. Nursing is a tertiary or service activity.
3. A food surplus is 'spare food' not needed by the farmer.
4. Farmers grow cotton to sell to make cloth.

Page 85 Quick Test

1. To get their products to market and import raw materials
2. Newly industrialising country
3. Possible examples include: computers, smartphones and TVs
4. Possible examples: Bluewater; Meadowhall; Trafford Centre; Metrocentre; Merry Hill

Page 87 Quick Test

1. Natural resources are created by nature.
2. They provide the food, materials and energy we need to survive.
3. Examples include: wood, fish, minerals, etc.
4. No – many are non-renewable; many of them will run out.

Page 89 Quick Test

1. Fish
2. Coal
3. Electricity
4. Norway, Netherlands and Qatar

Page 91 Quick Test

1. North
2. 2 cm by 2 cm
3. 1 km^2

Page 93 Quick Test

1. 10
2. 10 metres
3. Blue
4. Public house

Page 94: Rivers and Coasts

1. Upper; middle; lower [3]
2. a) Attrition; corrasion or abrasion; hydraulic action; solution [4]
    b) Waterfall (or any other landform where erosion is the dominant process, e.g. potholes; rapids) [1]
    c) Floodplains or levées [1]
3. Saturated soils; heavy rain; impermeable rock = physical cause [3]
    Urbanisation and deforestation = Human cause [2]
4. Different types of rock [1] will erode at different rates due to variations in resistance/strength [1].
5. Swash is more powerful than backwash in constructive waves [1]. Backwash is more powerful than swash in destructive waves [1].
6. Soft rock – sandstone [1]; hard rock – chalk, granite [2]
7. Longshore drift [1]
8. Residents and tourists [1]. Residents may wish to use hard engineering to protect their homes and businesses effectively and immediately [1]. Tourists may disagree because hard engineering, such as sea walls, can limit their enjoyment of the area [1].

Page 95: Landscapes

1. a) To use the world's resources [1] for your own gain/benefit [1]

b) Any two suitable examples: cutting down trees/ deforestation [1]; digging mines/quarries for coal [1]; controlling rivers for electricity [1]
2. Any three points from: the demand for space grows [1] and demand for resources grows [1]; more fragile landscapes are exploited [1]; land cannot support growing populations [1]; unsustainable [1]
3. a) Carbon dioxide [1]
   b) It is a greenhouse gas [1]
4. a) Increased dry periods [1] and less rainfall [1]
   b) Infertile [1] and unproductive [1]
5. a) Soil is unprotected from heavy rain [1] meaning it is washed away/eroded [1]
   b) Trees protect the soil from heavy rain [1] and roots bind the soil together [1]
6. a) Any two from: increased demand for space [1]; fuel [1]; resources found in rainforests [1]
   b) Originating and living/occurring naturally [1] in an area or environment [1]
   c) Can teach valuable lessons about how to manage these areas sustainably [1]; hold important information about ecology/medicinal plants [1]; are ancient peoples that have the right to live in their ancestral land [1]

Page 96: Population
1. a) The global birth rate is more than double the global death rate [1] so there are lots of extra people per year [1].
   b) As the birth rate is falling in almost every country [1], eventually the birth rate and the death rate will be the same [1] and so the world population will stop growing [1].
2. Examples: Sahara Desert – too dry; Himalayas – too mountainous; Antarctica – too cold (Any two plus reason for [4])
3. London [1] has the highest population density (5700 people per square kilometre) compared to the Highlands (8 people per square kilometre) [1].
4. In a civil war, families leave their homes and flee to another country [1] to be safe from the fighting [1].
5. Falling [1]
6. Many HICs have high death rates as unhealthy lifestyles [1] lead to high rates of obesity, cancer and heart disease ([1] for an example).
7. There is freedom of movement within the European Union [1] and they may be able to secure better paid jobs in another EU country [1].

Page 97: Urbanisation
1. a) High income country [1]; low income country [1]
   b) Low income countries [1]
2. a) As technology and transport improved [1], people began to move away from cities to live [1] and work [1].
   b) Suburbanisation [1] and counterurbanisation [1]
3. a) Crime [1]; abandoned shops [1]; derelict factories [1]
   b) A process aimed at attracting people [1] and businesses back to city centres [1]; Example: derelict factories are converted into flats and offices [1].
4. a) A city with over 10 million people [1]
   b) LICs [1]
5. People/society [1]; environment [1]; economy [1]
6. Solar panels [1] and well insulated homes [1] mean less energy [1] from burning fossil fuels is used [1].

> **Pages 98–101 Practice Questions**

Page 98: Development
1. a) Development measures how advanced a country is [1].
   b) Any two from: social; economic; environmental; cultural; technological [2]
   c) Any three from: life expectancy; infant mortality; literacy rates; birth rate; access to clean water [3]
   d) Any two from: Gross Domestic Product (GDP); GDP per capita; percentage of people working in different sectors [2]

2. Primary industries dominate in LICs [1]; for example fishing [1], farming [1], mining [1]
3. Severe climatic conditions such as drought [1] leave soils infertile and unproductive [1], for example in the Sahel. Natural hazards such as floods or earthquakes [1] mean money must be spent on recovering from these disasters [1], for example in Bangladesh.
4. The Brandt Line is misleading and outdated [1] because many countries below the line are in fact NICs (India and China) [1].
5. Because it shows the connection between economic and social development [1]; (plus [3] for considering why this is useful, for example, helps us to consider the human and physical factors that may affect development; allows us to assist development in a more appropriate way).
6. Attached [1]; donor [1]; recipient [1]; environment [1]; Corrupt [1]; dependency [1]
7. a) Sustainable development aims to help present and future generations [1]. If this to be successful then money must form just one part of the development process [1]. Economic sustainability [1], social sustainability [1] and environmental sustainability [1] must all be considered.
   b) Fair trade contributes to sustainable development by assisting social, environmental and economic progress. (Five marks for reference to how farmer; local community; environment; and local economy are assisted.) [5]

Page 99: Economic Activity
1. Companies carry out economic activities to make a profit [1].
2. Market researcher = quaternary [1]; teacher = tertiary [1]; coal miner = primary [1]; baker = secondary [1]
3. a) Primary workers obtain natural resources from the ground or the sea, such as fish, coal, iron, wood [2].
   b) Any two examples: nurse; teacher; lawyer; shop assistant [2]
   c) A = 70% [1]; B = 28% [1]; C = 80% [1]
4. a) Any two examples: strawberries; asparagus; sweetcorn; green beans; apples [2]
   b) About 60% [1]
5. natural resources [2]; energy [1]
6. a) Any two from: India; Bangladesh; China [2]
   b) A 'sweatshop' factory is one that has poor working conditions [1], such as long hours or low wages [1].
7. Office cleaner [1]; security guard [1]

Page 100: Natural Resources
1. Natural resources are found in nature [1].
2. Using resources sustainably means using them carefully so they will last longer [1] and be available to future generations [1].
3. They will eventually run out [1].
4. Any two suitable points: it can be used as a fuel [1] or for building [1] or for making paper [1].
5. a) 25–30 years [1]
   b) Coniferous trees are quick growing [1] so it is easy to plant new trees to replace those that are cut down [1].
6. a) Mahogany or teak [1]
   b) Preserving the rainforest prevents it being chopped down [1] and ensures rainforest wildlife do not lose their habitat [1].
7. a) A fish farm is an artificial method [1] of growing fish for humans to eat [1].
   b) On a factory ship fish are processed [1] and frozen [1] at sea.
8. Natural gas is used in homes for heating [1] and cooking [1].

Page 101: Ordnance Survey Maps
1. a) i) 7857 [1] ii) 7559 [1]
   b) i) St Newlyn East [1] ii) Holywell [1]
   c) 1.8 to 1.9 km [1]

> **Pages 103–109 Revise Questions**

Page 103 Quick Test
1. Geographic Information System
2. The police use a GIS for plotting crime data on a digital map
3. A line on a digital map might show a road or river
4. Digital maps in the UK are produced by the Ordnance Survey

Page 105 Quick Test
1. Geographical Technology
2. Google Earth
3. In the Layers Panel you can switch different layers of information on or off.
4. A satellite is an orbiting spacecraft that carries cameras and other equipment.

Page 107 Quick Test
1. Learning Outside the Classroom
2. Co-operation is important because fieldwork involves group work
3. A grid reference is an example of co-ordinates used on a map
4. A wind vane is used to record wind direction

Page 109 Quick Test
1. Ordnance Survey
2. A fieldwork sketch is a drawing done outside during fieldwork
3. 75% use public transport (the bus)
4. A graph that uses pictures or symbols

Pages 110–111 Practice Questions

Page 110: Geographic Information Systems
1. Hardware [1], software [1] and digital data [1]
2. A GIS can be used to view data on maps [1].
3. a) Plotting crime data on a GIS provides a visual record that shows patterns of crime [1] and allows the police to target specific areas [1].
   b) One from: ambulance service; water; gas and electricity suppliers; supermarkets [1]
4. So that you can see the layer beneath [1]
5. a) Things that occur at a particular point are shown as symbols, e.g. the altitude of a mountain [1].
   b) Information such as roads, rivers and railway lines are shown as lines on a GIS layer [1].
6. You cannot add data on most online GIS [1].
   You cannot change data on most online GIS [1].
7. Any two examples: information about leisure facilities; waste disposal facilities; parks and open spaces; local footpaths; shopping centres [2]
8. a) Google Earth is a virtual globe [1] with maps and other data shown as layers [1].
   b) By using the zoom tool [1] to move from viewing on the global scale [1], through the national scale [1] to the local scale [1].
9. a) Any two suitable examples: On a satellite image you can see settlements [1], roads [1] and land use [1].
   b) Aerial photos [1]

Page 111: Fieldwork
1. a) Learning Outside the Classroom (LOtC) [1]
   b) Outdoors = Taking photos; Conducting Surveys [2]. In the classroom = Displaying data; Analysing data; Drawing conclusions [3]
   c) Fieldwork can involve bad weather [1] and working in difficult environments, e.g. slippery rocks [1].
2. If you are not accurate, the results will be incorrect [1] and you could come to the wrong conclusion [1].
3. Two from: types of shops; number of pedestrians; size of shop frontage [2]
4. To measure the speed [1] of a stream or river [1]
5. Closed question [1]
6. You might use a historical map when presenting your fieldwork data to show how something has changed [1] over time [1].
7. a) If you were showing different amounts of something [1] in different categories [1]
   b) A pictogram is a visual way of presenting data [1].

Pages 112–117 Review Questions

Page 112: Development
1. a) Low income countries [1]
   b) Any suitable example, e.g. Ethiopia [1]
2. Levels of health [1] and education [1]

3. The average [1] age a person will live to [1]
4. Possible answers: manufacturing; processing; construction [1]
5. Newly industrialising country [1]
6. Because the value of their exports is less than that of their imports [1], and they spend much of their GDP repaying loans [1] borrowed from HICs [1].
7. Child health [1]; Reduced child mortality [1]; An end to poverty [1]; Universal education [1]
8. Sustainable development is development that meets the needs of the present [1] without compromising the ability of future generations [1] to meet their own needs [1].

Page 113: Economic Activity
1. Primary [1]; secondary [1]; tertiary [1]; quaternary [1]
2. Manufacture means to make something in a factory [1].
3. a) Take it to market [1] to sell and earn money [1]
   b) It usually ends up in HICs [1] such as the UK or USA [1].
4. a) Any two points: Farmers use chemicals to make crops grow [1], to kill pests [1] or to stop the spread of disease [1].
   b) An arable farm grows crops [1] and a pastoral farm rears animals [1].
5. Machines [1]
6. a) In the UK we make cars, clothes, chemicals and food products in factories. ([2] for two examples.)
   b) A TV [1]; a smartphone [1]
7. Samsung [1]

Page 114: Natural Resources
1. They can last indefinitely [1] if they are used in a sustainable way [1].
2. We use them again [1]. Glass bottles or metal cans can be recycled [1].
3. a) Softwood trees [1]
   b) Over 100 years [1]
   c) So that local people can have jobs [1] and so wood can be exported so that the government earns money [1].
4. a) Any two examples: humans collect fish, shellfish, prawns, seaweed, coral and salt from the sea [1]
   b) Overfishing results in fish stocks declining [1] as there are not enough fish left to breed [1].
5. a) Less than 3% [1]
   b) It causes pollution [1], including greenhouse gases that cause global warming [1].
6. a) Oil is not an important fuel in our power stations [1].
   b) Fertilisers [1]; pesticides [1]

Page 115: Ordnance Survey Maps
1. a) Six-figure grid references give the location of a square that is 100 m × 100 m [1]; a four-figure grid reference gives the location of a square 1 km × 1 km [1].
   b) i) 802553 or 802554 [2] ii) 787537 or 788538 [2]
   c) i) Church (with a steeple) [2] ii) caravan/camp site [2] iii) tourist information [2]
   d) i) 833559 [2] ii) 838554 [2] iii) 832552 [2]

Page 116: Geographic Information Systems
1. It helps to decide which vehicle to send to answer an emergency call [1].
2. a) A GIS layer shows a set of information [1]. It could be land use, settlement, roads or relief [1].
   b) You might switch a layer off if it wasn't relevant to your work [1] or you could switch a layer on if you wanted to analyse some new information [1].
   c) A map [1]
   d) Photo or satellite image [1]
3. Buildings or areas such as lakes or forests or towns [1]
4. Text is needed on a GIS layer to add names to the locations and features on a map [1].
5. Allow you to fly automatically from one part of the world to another [1]. You can also fly under the sea and view the ocean floor [1].

Page 117: Fieldwork
1. a) In the school grounds [1]; in the local neighbourhood [1]
   b) Data collection is the part of the fieldwork process carried out in the field [1].

2. It is important because there are many things that could go wrong or be dangerous if people were not safety conscious [1].
3. A georeferenced photo is one that has the co-ordinates recorded [1] so that you know where it was taken [1].
4. Any two examples: width of beach; pebble size; types of waves [2]
5. a) An anonymous questionnaire is one where the name of the person answering the questions is not recorded [1].
   b) An example might be: Which is your favourite take-away food? or a similar question with no choice of answers given [2].
6. A choropleth map
7. a)

| 60% | 23% | 12% | 5% | [4]

   b)

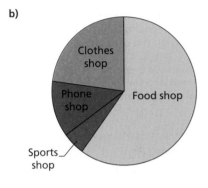

[4]

Pages 118–130 Mixed Test-Style Questions

1. a) Individuals carry out economic activities or work in order to earn money [1]. Companies carry out economic activities or business in order to make a profit [1].
   b) People are involved in getting natural resources [1] from the ground [1] or from the sea [1].
   c) i) True [1] ii) False [1] iii) False [1]
2. a) India [1] b) China [1] c) Russia [1]
3. a) Examples: low GDP per capita: South Korea $872, Kenya $2007 [1]; lack of education: Kenya today has 78–85% adult literacy [1]; high proportion of people working in agriculture: Kenya today has over 40% of its population in the sector [1]
   b) Any three from: rich country, $31 489 GDP per capita [1]; 10th largest economy in the world [1]; employment in high-tech industry, companies like Samsung and LG [1]; high quality education [1]; it is a democracy [1]
4. a) Any three from: corrasion (abrasion) [1]; attrition [1]; hydraulic action [1]; solution [1]
   b) i) Middle [1] ii) Upper [1] iii) Lower [1]
5. Non-renewable resources such as coal [1] are those natural resources which have taken millions of years to form and which will eventually run out [1]. Renewable resources such as copper [1] are those that can be recycled so that they can be used again [1] or some natural resources such as trees can be grown to replace those cut down [1].
6. One argument for cutting down the trees in a rainforest is that it provides jobs for local people [1]. They need money to buy food and other goods [1]. One argument for not chopping down the trees in the rainforest is that the trees provide a natural habitat for wild animals [1] and without it, those wild animals will die [1].
7. a) Nile [1]; Euphrates [1]; Tigris [1]
   b) Any two from: water supply [1]; useful for transport [1] and/ or trade [1]; fertile land due to silt left from flood water [1]
   c) Oil [1]; not every country has oil reserves [1]
8. a) Granite = C [1]; sandstone = A [1]; Chalk = B [1]
   b) Igneous rocks are hard/resistant to weathering/erosion [1]; contain mineral crystals [1]; are non-porous [1]
9. The process [1] by which the proportion of people living in towns and cities grows [1] (Must have word 'process' for [2])
10. 'Per capita' means 'per person' / for each person in the population [1]

11.

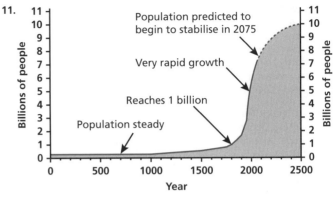

([2] for correctly labelled axes; [2] for correct graph; [2] for any two of annotations) [6]
12. The climate is usually not suitable [1], e.g. it may be too cold [1] or there may be few resources [1] that humans need, e.g. food [1].
13. a) Cold deserts: Gobi, Taklamakan (Any one for [1]); Hot deserts: Thar, Arabian, Rub' al-Khali, Sahara (Any one for [1])
   b) Similarities: Both types have low rainfall (precipitation) [1], e.g. Gobi = 194 mm a year, Arabian and Rub' al-Khali = less than 30 mm a year. [1] Differences: cold deserts have low temperatures during the daytime, e.g. Gobi = –40°C [1], whereas hot deserts have very high daytime temperatures, e.g. Thar = 50°C [1]
14. Tropical rainforests [1]; savannah grasslands [1]
15. a) If two plates move towards each other, this is called a destructive plate boundary [1]. At this boundary the rocks in the Earth's crust are heated and squeezed by great pressure [1] and pushed upwards to form mountains [1].
   b) Conservative plate boundary [1]
16. a) Biological weathering [1]
   b) Happens in cold, mountainous areas = Freeze-thaw weathering [1]
      Often occurs in deserts due to temperature change = Onion-skin weathering [1]
      Takes place when weak acid in rainwater dissolves rocks = Chemical weathering [1]
      Occurs when plants and animals break down rocks = Biological weathering [1]
17. a) Processes of weathering and erosion will carve out the glaciated landscape [1]. (Explanation of at least two forms of weathering/erosion for extra [3] – freeze-thaw, plucking, abrasion)
   b) Any one from: drumlin; moraine [1]
18. Any three suitable points: Some urban centres are used less and less for shopping and business [1], so derelict factories, abandoned shops, poor quality housing, unemployment, crime and a poor environment remain [1]. This is not an attractive place for people to live/work/shop [1].
19. Rain is small droplets of liquid water [1]. Hail is pellets of solid ice [1]. Snow is made of tiny ice crystals arranged in patterns to form a snowflake [1]. Sleet is partly melted snow so is a mixture of ice and water [1].
20. Wind speed [1] using an anemometer [1] and wind direction [1] using a wind vane [1]
21. a) Ploughed field [1]
    b) Trees and plants act as umbrellas and intercept rainfall before it hits the ground [1]. Tree and plant roots hold the soil together so that it is harder to wash away [1]. Trees act as windbreaks and reduce the effect of wind erosion on the soil [1]. Trees and plants store water from the ground, which reduces the amount of water available to flow over the soil surface [1].
    c) Contour ploughing [1]; Building terraced fields [1]; Planting trees [1]
22. Examples: Through tourism – 180 000 UK tourists visited Kenya in 2019 [1]; Through tea – Brooke Bond owns and runs tea plantations in Kenya, and the tea is sold in UK shops [1]; Through flowers – Kenyan flowers are sold in most UK supermarkets [1]

23. **a)** They tell us about evolution **[1]**. Each part of the Geological Timescale has a set of rocks that contain particular plants or animals that lived at a certain time in the past **[1]** and the fossils help us to identify the age of the rocks and where they belong in the timescale **[1]**.

b) Fish **[1]**; Dinosaurs **[1]**; Birds **[1]**; Humans **[1]**

24. Global temperatures fall (everywhere becomes cooler) **[1]**. This results in more precipitation falling as snow in both temperate and polar areas **[1]**. As the snow builds up, it forms glaciers and ice sheets that cover the land **[1]**. As less water returns to the oceans, sea levels fall **[1]**.

25. Rural-to-urban migration **[1]** means many people are moving to cities for work **[1]**; poorer countries are unable to provide home for these immigrants **[1]** who are forced to live in makeshift housing **[1]** close to the city. Due to the high rate of rural-to-urban migration in LICs, shanty towns grow larger **[1]**.

26. **a)** Fieldwork is a process that involves several different stages **[1]**. Collecting data when out on fieldwork is an important first stage **[1]**. This data can then be used as evidence to answer fieldwork questions. The data can be presented as graphs or added to maps **[1]**. These can then be analysed so that fieldwork questions can be answered **[1]**.

b) Examples: the type of shop or service using a simple classification; the number of different floors in each building; the condition of the building; the size of the shop front; the number of people entering the business per hour. (**[1]** per example to a maximum of **[4]**)

27. Any four suitable points: the temperature **[1]** using a thermometer **[1]** and the wind speed **[1]** using an anemometer **[1]**; you might also record areas of shade and sunshine **[1]** on a map **[1]**.

28. **a)** Building dams **[1]**; Creating reservoirs **[1]**

b) One advantage and one disadvantage of soft engineering and one advantage and one disadvantage of hard engineering for **[4]**
Examples:
Advantages of hard engineering: groynes stop longshore drift carrying beach material away **[1]**; sea walls effectively reflect wave energy from eroding coast **[1]**
Disadvantages: expensive to maintain **[1]**; can look unattractive **[1]**

Advantages of soft engineering: beach nourishment is a more natural-looking method of coastal defence **[1]**; cheaper and more sustainable in the long term **[1]**
Disadvantages: can be less effective **[1]**; managed retreat means valuable land may be lost **[1]**.

29. **a)** A GIS has many practical uses that can help people in real life **[1]**. It can make their job easier or safer or more effective **[1]**. The sorts of people that use GIS include transport companies, the police and other emergency services **[1]**. The police might use it to plot details of crimes that have taken place in particular locations **[1]**.

b) You can have as many layers as you like in a GIS as it is possible to switch them off **[1]** if you don't want to see them or switch them on **[1]** when you want to use the information.

c) A line is a linear feature **[1]**, such as a river or road or railway **[1]**, whereas a point is a feature found at a single location **[1]**, such as a mountain peak or a building **[1]**.

30. Concerns to include five key issues: honeypot site attracting too many tourists **[1]**; overuse of footpaths leading to soil erosion **[1]**; dogs scaring/worrying the animals **[1]**; tourists leaving gates open meaning livestock get loose **[1]**; noise and water pollution in the lakes **[1]**

31. Because workers are paid less so this makes the goods cheaper **[1]** or because they are able to produce goods on a large scale to keep prices down **[1]**.

32. Most volcanoes give warning signs before they erupt **[1]**, which gives people time to evacuate the area and move to a safe place **[1]**. Earthquakes happen very suddenly and without warning / It is not possible to accurately predict earthquakes **[1]**.

33. The tropical climate and the desert climate both have very high temperatures all year round **[1]** but the tropical climate has a high rainfall **[1]** whereas the desert climate has little or no rainfall throughout the year **[1]**.

Glossary

a

ablation   when glacial ice melts

abrasion   when stones carried in the water scrape the river bed and banks

accumulation   when a glacier increases in size due to increased snowfall and less melting

aerial photo   a photo taken from the air, usually from an aeroplane

ageing population   a population that has a large and growing number of old people

agroforestry   growing trees and crops together

air pressure   the pressure resulting from the weight of the Earth's atmosphere

alpine tundra   environmental region found in upland areas where the ground is frozen all year and trees do not grow

altitude   the height of the land above sea level

Arab   member of an ethnic group originating in the Arabian Peninsula

Arabic   language spoken by Arabs

arable   a farm that grows crops such as wheat or potatoes

arch   a rock formation created from erosion and weathering

b

bar chart   a graph that uses vertical or horizontal bars of equal width to represent frequency

bedrock   solid rock found below soil that cannot be dug out by hand

bi-polar scale   a type of rating scale with a continuum between two opposite end points or opinions

birth rate   the number of babies born per 1000 people per year in a particular country or area

Brandt Line   an imaginary line on a map of the world dividing the wealthier countries (above) and poorer countries (below)

British Empire   the countries and regions of the world that were once colonies of Great Britain

brown earth   type of soil found in the UK which is 1–2 metres deep with a thick topsoil layer

c

carbonation   the process by which limestone rock is weathered; weak acid in rainwater reacts with calcium carbonate in the rock to form soluble minerals that are then washed away

carbon sink   a natural store for carbon, e.g. rainforests

cardinal points   the four points of a compass: north, south, east and west

carrying capacity   the maximum number of people that the land can support

catchment area   area of land from which the rainfall drains into a particular river

chaebol   large South Korean company that produces a range of goods and services

chernozem   dark-coloured, fertile soil found in steppe regions

climate   the pattern of average temperature and average rainfall across the year

climate graph   a graph that combines data for temperature and rainfall at a particular location

climate zone   areas of the world that have the same pattern of temperature and rainfall

cold desert   environmental region of very low rainfall and low average daily temperatures

colony   group of people or country that is under the control of or occupied by settlers from another country

Communist   someone who holds the political belief that everything should belong to and be run by the government in order to create a fair and equal society

compass   device for determining the location of magnetic north or a diagram on a map showing the direction of north, south, east and west

conservative boundary   a plate boundary where two plates on the Earth's crust are sliding past each other

constructive boundary   a plate boundary where two plates on the Earth's crust are moving away from each other and new crust is being created from material rising up from the mantle

contour line   line joining points of equal height on a map

core   the very hot centre of the Earth

counterurbanisation   the movement of people from urban areas to smaller towns and villages

crust   the relatively thin layer of rocks that forms the outermost layer of the Earth

crystalline   minerals found in rocks that have a regular geometric shape

d

data   information that is collected during fieldwork activities

death rate   the number of deaths per 1000 people per year in a particular country or area

debt   when money is owed

deciduous   trees that lose their leaves in the autumn

deforestation   cutting down and removing of trees from an area

democracy   a political system where citizens have the right to vote for the government of the country

dense population   an area that has a relatively large number of people living there

dependency   to rely on another country as a main source of income

deposition   the process of transported material being deposited

desert climate   a climate with high temperatures all year round and little or no rainfall

desertification   the process by which land becomes infertile and unproductive desert, useless for farming

destructive boundary   a plate boundary where two plates on the Earth's crust meet and one is destroyed as it moves beneath the other

differential erosion   erosion that happens at different rates (caused by the differing hardness/resistance of the rock types)

discordant   describes bands of different rocks

donor   a country that gives aid

dormant   describes a volcano that has not erupted in living memory but may erupt again in the future

drumlin   a tear-shaped hill formed by glacial deposition

e

earthquake   a violent shaking of the Earth's crust caused by plate movement

emigrants   people who move out of a country

enquiry-based learning   learning by asking questions and trying to find answers

epicentre   the point where the shockwaves of an earthquake reach the surface of the Earth and cause maximum damage

Equator   an imaginary line drawn around the Earth at 0° latitude separating the northern and southern hemispheres

erosion   the removal of weathered material by the action of wind, water or ice

erratic   a large rock or boulder deposited far from its place of origin after glacial melt

ethnic group   people of the same race or nationality who share a particular culture

evolution   changes in living things over millions of years as they adapt to their changing environment

extinct   a plant or living creature that has died out; a volcano that will not erupt again

extrusive   igneous rocks that are formed on the surface of the Earth

f

factory ship   a very large ship that accompanies fishing boats then processes, freezes and stores the fish

fair trade   ensures that trade is beneficial to an LIC and not controlled unfairly by the HICs it trades with

family planning   advice about contraception and managing the number of children born

fieldwork   teaching and learning outside the classroom, usually away from the school

firn   a dense and compacted body of snow

fish farm   a place where fish are artificially bred and grown for human use

floodplain   an area of flat land bordering a river

focus   the point where an earthquake starts, usually deep underground

fossil   the remains of a living creature or plant trapped in a sedimentary rock

fossil fuel   a fuel formed from plants (coal) or ocean micro-organisms (oil and natural gas) trapped in sedimentary rock

freeze-thaw weathering   breaking up of rocks by water freezing and expanding in cracks

g

Geographic Information System (GIS)   a system consisting of hardware, software and data that allows geographical information to be plotted on maps and then studied

Geological Timescale   a timescale that shows when rocks and fossils were formed

georeference   co-ordinates for a location so that it can be plotted on a map

geotechnology   technology that uses georeferenced data to create maps

glacial period   a period of cooling within an ice age

glaciation   a major cooling of the Earth leading to the formation of ice sheets that cover large areas

global warming   climate change in which the average temperature across the world increases

greenhouse gases   gases that trap heat, preventing it from escaping back into space

grid lines   lines drawn on OS maps running north to south and east to west

grid reference   a four- or six-figure number used to locate places on a map

Gross Domestic Product (GDP)   total value of goods and services produced by a country in one year

h

hard engineering   the use of artificial materials to change the natural flow of a river

high income country (HIC)   a country with a gross national income per capita of US$13 205 or more in 2022

high-tech   using computers and other modern technology to make products such as phones, cameras and medical equipment

historical map   an old map that shows what the geography looked like in the past

honeypot   a tourist site that attracts large numbers of visitors

horizons   the layers found in soil

hot desert   environmental region with very low rainfall and high average daily temperatures

Human Development Index (HDI)   a composite indicator for development; measures life expectancy, knowledge and standard of living

humidity   the amount of moisture (water) in the air

humid sub-tropical   environmental region found just north of the Tropic of Cancer and just south of the Tropic of Capricorn where the air is warm and holds a high percentage of moisture

humus   organic matter found in soil formed from decayed plants and animals

i

ice age   a time of extreme cooling of the Earth's climate where sheets of ice cover large areas of land

igneous   rocks formed from molten rock (magma)

immigrants   people who move into a country

independence   the act of a country separating from a colonial power and becoming self-governing

indicators   used to measure and compare levels of development

indigenous   people who have historical ties to a particular area

interglacial period   a period of warmer climate within an ice age

intrusive   igneous rocks that are formed beneath the surface of the Earth

Islam   religion founded by the prophet Mohammed whose teachings are written in the Koran

l

labour   workers in a factory or other type of business

latosol   type of soil found in tropical regions which is 20–30 metres deep with a very thin topsoil layer

layer of information   a single set of information within a GIS

leaching   washing of minerals and nutrients through soil by water

Learning Outside the Classroom (LOtC)   any kind of learning that happens outside the classroom

levée   a natural deposit of sand and mud alongside a river

line   a symbol that shows things like roads and rivers on a GIS

line graph   a graph that plots points and then joins them up to form a line

lithified   the process of sediments becoming sedimentary rocks

longshore drift   the process of beach material being moved laterally due to the waves meeting the shore at a certain angle

low income country (LIC)   a developing country with a gross national income per capita of US$1085 or less in 2022; many are found in Africa

m

mantle   the hot, semi-molten layer of rock that surrounds the Earth's core

manufacturing   making a product in a factory or workshop

maximum temperature   the highest recorded temperature in a day, month or year

meander   a curve or bend in a river

mechanised   the use of machinery to do work in factories or on farms

Mediterranean climate   climate characterised by hot, dry summers and warm, wet winters

megacity   a city with a population of 10 million or more

metamorphic   rocks that have been formed from igneous or sedimentary rocks subjected to heat and pressure

migration   the movement of people from one area or country to another area or country

mineral   a natural resource found in rock that is not made from plant or animal matter, e.g. gold, silver, diamond, quartz, salt

minimum temperature   the lowest recorded temperature in a day, month or year

monsoon   climate characterised by a definite wet season and dry season

montane forest   tropical rainforest found in upland areas where there is very high humidity

moraine   the material deposited after a glacier has melted

Muslim   a follower of Islam

n

natural resources   materials that come from the land or sea which humans use to make products

newly industrialising countries (NICs)   countries such as China and Brazil that have developed industries, often making products for HICs; countries experiencing rapid economic growth

nomadic pastoralists   traditional farmers who herd livestock from one place to another in search of water and grass

non-porous   rocks that do not hold water

non-renewable   a natural resource that cannot be replaced and will eventually run out

o

ocean current   a warm or cold flow of ocean water that moves long distances and affects climate

One Child Policy   introduced in China as a means of controlling population growth in 1979, it limited every family to having one child only

onion-skin weathering   splitting and flaking of a rock surface due to repeated heating and cooling

Ordnance Survey   the organisation that produces the maps that are most widely used in the UK

overfishing   catching too many fish so that there are not enough to breed naturally

p

parent material   the type of rock that soil has been weathered from

pastoral   a farm where animals such as cattle or sheep are reared

perception   what we think about something (our opinion)

permafrost   ground found in tundra regions where the subsoil is frozen all year round

pictogram   a graph that uses pictures or symbols to represent data

plate boundary   the line along which two tectonic plates meet

plucking   when rocks become frozen to and removed by a glacier

point   a particular location on a digital map

polar climate   a climate with low rainfall and low temperatures throughout the year

polygon   a series of locations that can be joined together to enclose an area of any shape on a GIS

population density   a statistic showing the number of people living in a square kilometre of land

population distribution   the way in which people are spread across the world or a particular area

population growth   the increase in the number of people in a particular country or area

porous   rocks that are able to hold water

poverty   a lack of money to buy the essential things that people need to live

power station   a place where electricity is generated by using fuel to heat water and power turbines

precipitation   different types of water that fall from clouds (rain, hail, sleet and snow)

primary activity   a job that involves obtaining natural resources from the land or sea

q

quality of life   a statistic that measures people's ability to buy or find enough resources to meet their daily needs

quaternary activity   work that involves collecting, processing, analysing and providing information

r

raw data   data that hasn't been processed or altered in any way

reaforrestation   when trees are planted in deforested areas

recipient   a country receiving an aid donation

recycle   use resources again and again to extend their life

refugees   people who flee from their own country due to war or natural disasters

relief   the shape of the land

renewable   a natural resource that can be replaced so it is always around

retail   shops selling goods and services

retreat   when glaciers melt and decrease in size owing to warmer temperatures

Richter scale   a measure of the energy released (magnitude or size) by an earthquake

rural-to-urban migration the process of people moving from the countryside into towns and cities

S

satellite imagery photos of the Earth taken from space taken by a satellite

savannah grasslands environmental region of grassland with few trees found in tropical and sub-tropical countries

scale lines lines drawn on the edge of a map to indicate how far a distance on the map is in reality

sea level the point where the land meets the sea

secondary activity a job that involves making a product, often in a factory

sedimentary rocks formed from deposits that are originally from older rocks and living organisms

self-help scheme a scheme giving local people ownership of land and tools, and offering help to improve their own living conditions

semi-arid environmental region with little rainfall, usually 200–500 mm a year

service an activity that helps people or organisations in some way

shanty town an area of makeshift housing built on unwanted land on the outskirts of a city

snout the end of a glacier at any given point in time

soft engineering the use of natural measures to reduce flood risk

soil erosion the removal of soil from the landscape by the action of wind and water

sparse population an area that has relatively few people living there

spot height point on a map indicating the height above sea level

stack a rock formation caused by erosion; formed when an arch collapses

steppe environmental region found in northern Europe and Asia consisting of grassland and few trees

stump a rock formation caused by erosion; formed when an arch collapses to leave a stack and the stack reduces in size

subsoil soil that is found below topsoil

sub-tropical environmental region located just north of the Tropic of Cancer or just south of the Tropic of Capricorn

suburbanisation the growth and development of residential areas just outside towns and cities

sustainable careful use of resources so that we have enough for now and for future generations

sustainable city a city that offers a good quality of life for residents, without compromising the quality of life for future residents

sustainable development development that meets the needs of present generations without compromising the ability of future generations to meet their own needs

t

taiga environmental region of evergreen, coniferous forests

tectonic plate a section of the Earth's crust

temperate climate a climate that has moderate rainfall with cold/mild winters and cool/warm summers

temperature range the difference between the maximum and minimum temperatures

terracing building fields up in steps on a slope to enable farming to take place and to minimise erosion

tertiary activity a job that involves providing a service to individuals or companies

textiles cloth made from natural or artificial fibres and usually used to make clothes

topsoil the layer of soil on the surface of the ground

trade deficit more money is spent on buying goods (imports) than is made on selling goods (exports)

transportation the process of eroded material being carried along

triangulation point a reference point used by cartographers to draw maps accurately

tropical climate a climate that has high temperatures and high rainfall all year

tropical equatorial forest another name for tropical rainforest

tropical rainforest ecosystem consisting of a very high density of forest vegetation and wildlife found between latitude 28°N and 28°S

tropical typhoon large-scale low pressure system that develops in warm seas in the Indian and Pacific Oceans, characterised by strong winds and heavy rainfall

tropical wet environmental region either side of the Equator between latitude 23°N and 23°S with high levels of rainfall over 2500 mm

tsunami a large wave caused by an undersea earthquake

tundra an environmental region around the Arctic Circle where it is so cold that trees do not grow and the ground is frozen all year round

tundra climate a climate where temperatures are below freezing most of the year and the low level of precipitation falls mainly as snow

u

urban decline the decline of an urban area, characterised by unemployment, crime, poverty and poor quality housing

urbanisation the increase in the population in urban areas

urban regeneration the revival of a run-down urban area through investment

v

virtual globe a computer-generated image of the Earth

volcano a mountain formed when molten magma escapes from the mantle and flows as lava on the Earth's surface

w

waterfall a vertical drop where water flows over; part of a river or stream

wave-cut notch an indentation in the base of a cliff, where the waves have eroded it

wave-cut platform a sloping rock ledge at the base of a cliff, created by erosion

weather daily changes in the atmosphere that affect humans

weathering breakdown of rocks by the action of weather, water, chemicals and living things

working age the group of people in a population aged roughly 16–64 years

Index

Collins

KS3
Geography
Workbook

Adam Gibson and Tony Grundy

Contents

Rethink Revision

Have you ever taken part in a quiz and thought '*I know this*!', but no matter how hard you scrabbled around in your brain you just couldn't come up with the answer?

It's very frustrating when this happens, but in a fun situation it doesn't really matter. However, in tests and assessments, it is essential that you can recall the relevant information when you need to.

Most students think that revision is about making sure you **know** *stuff*, but it is also about being confident that you can **retain** that *stuff* over time and **recall** it when needed.

Revision that Really Works

Experts have found that there are two techniques that help with *all* of these things and consistently produce better results in tests and exams compared to other revision techniques.

Applying these techniques to your KS3 revision will ensure you get better results in tests and assessments and will have all the relevant knowledge at your fingertips when you start studying for your GCSEs.

It really isn't rocket science either – you simply need to:
- **test yourself** on each topic as many times as possible
- **leave a gap** between the test sessions.

It is most effective if you leave a good period of time between the test sessions, e.g. between a week and a month. The idea is that just as you start to forget the information, you force yourself to recall it again, keeping it fresh in your mind.

Three Essential Revision Tips

1 Use Your Time Wisely
- Allow yourself plenty of time.
- Try to start revising six months before tests and assessments – it's more effective and less stressful.
- Your revision time is precious so use it wisely – using the techniques described on this page will ensure you revise effectively and efficiently and get the best results.
- Don't waste time re-reading the same information over and over again – it's time-consuming and not effective!

2 Make a Plan
- Identify all the topics you need to revise (this Complete Revision & Practice book will help you).
- Plan at least five sessions for each topic.
- A one-hour session should be ample to test yourself on the key ideas for a topic.
- Spread out the practice sessions for each topic – the optimum time to leave between each session is about one month but, if this isn't possible, just make the gaps as big as realistically possible.

3 Test Yourself
- Methods for testing yourself include: quizzes, practice questions, flashcards, past papers, explaining a topic to someone else.
- This Complete Revision & Practice book gives you seven practice test opportunities per topic.
- Don't worry if you get an answer wrong – provided you check what the right answer is, you are more likely to get the same or similar questions right in future!

Visit our website to download your free flashcards, for more information about the benefits of these revision techniques and for further guidance on how to plan ahead and make them work for you.

collins.co.uk/collinsks3revision

Place Knowledge

Location Knowledge – Russia

1 a) i)–v) Complete the labels on the map to identify five seas that surround Russia. [5]

vi)–ix) Complete the labels on the map to show the location of these four cities:

Moscow   St Petersburg   Novosibirsk   Yekaterinburg [4]

b) Russia's largest lake is shown on the map. What is its name? _____ [1]

2 Russia has many natural resources, many of which it exports to other countries.

a) Give an example of a non-renewable natural resource. _____ [1]

b) Give an example of a resource that is a precious metal. _____ [1]

c) Give an example of a renewable natural resource. _____ [1]

d) What is the estimated value of Russian exports in $? $ _____ [1]

3 a) Describe the Steppe region.

_____

_____ [2]

b) Explain why the Steppe region is important for Russia.

_____

_____

_____ [2]

Total Marks _____ / 18

Location Knowledge – China

4 **a) i)–v)** Complete the labels on the map to identify five countries that border or are close neighbours of China. [5]

vi)–ix) Complete the labels on the map to show the location of these four cities:

Shanghai Wuhan Shenzen Xi'an [4]

b) Name the two deserts shown on the map. .... and .... [2]

5 Describe how China's One Child Policy has changed since 2015.

....

.... [3]

6 Explain why China's tropical rainforest area is environmentally important.

....

.... [2]

7 Describe China's political system.

....

.... [2]

Total Marks .... / 18

Place Knowledge

Location Knowledge – India

1 **a)** **i)–iv)** Complete the labels on the map to identify four countries that border or are close neighbours of India. [4]

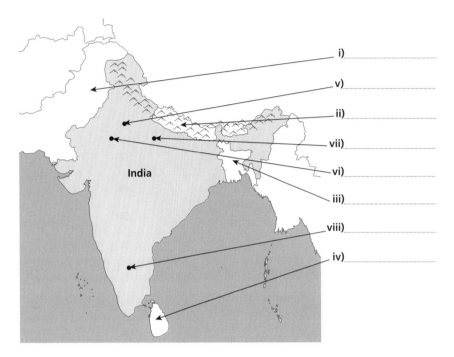

v)–viii) Complete the labels on the map to show the location of these four cities:

New Delhi   **Jaipur**   **Bengaluru (Bangalore)**   **Lucknow** [4]

b) Name the mountain range shown on the map. .... [1]

c) Name the two sea areas shown on the map. .... and .... [2]

2 **a)** Name an export crop grown in the semi-arid region of the Deccan Plateau. .... [1]

b) Give **two** examples of both secondary (manufacturing) and tertiary (services) industries in India.

....

.... [4]

3 Describe India's annual monsoon climate pattern.

....

....

.... [4]

Total Marks .... / 20

Location Knowledge – The Middle East

4 **i)–v)** Complete the labels on the map to identify five countries in the Middle East. [5]

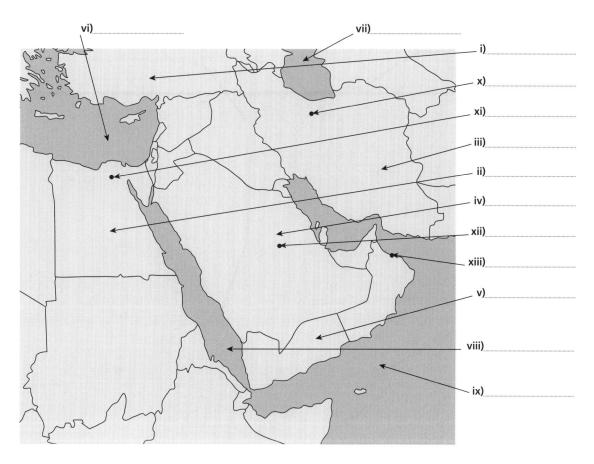

vi)–ix) Complete the labels to identify the four seas marked on the map. [4]

x)–xiii) Complete the labels on the map to show the location of these four cities:

     Cairo   **Riyadh**   **Muscat**   **Tehran** [4]

5 Name the two climate types in the Middle East. _____ and _____ [2]

6 Name the most valuable export from the Middle East. _____ [1]

7 **a)** State the names of the countries with the lowest and highest GDP per capita in the Middle East.

_____

_____ [2]

b) Give the approximate total GDP for the Middle East. $ _____ [1]

Total Marks _____ / 19

Place Knowledge

Africa and Asia Compared – Kenya

1 **i)–v)** Complete the labels on the map to identify the five countries that border Kenya. [5]

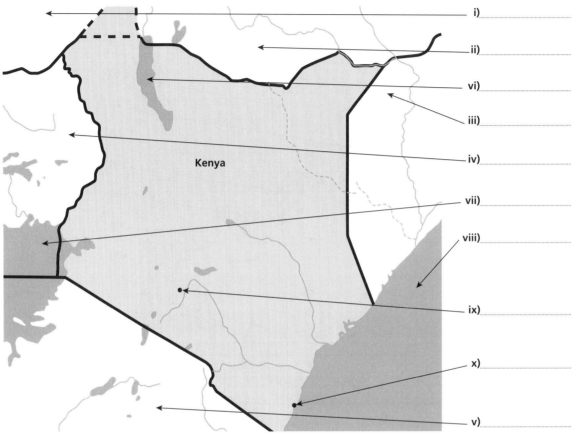

i) ....

ii) ....

vi) ....

iii) ....

iv) ....

vii) ....

viii) ....

ix) ....

x) ....

v) ....

vi)–viii) Complete the labels to identify the lakes and sea shown on the map. [3]

ix)–x) Complete the labels to identify the capital and the port city shown on the map. [2]

2 Describe Kenya's exports.

....

....

....

[4]

3 Who are the Maasai? .... [1]

4 Tourism accounts for 25% of Kenya's earnings. Describe why Kenya is popular with tourists.

....

....

....

[4]

Total Marks .... / 19

Africa and Asia Compared – South Korea

5 **i)–iii)** Complete the labels on the map to identify three close neighbours of South Korea. [3]

i)
ii)
v)
vii)
viii)
South Korea
ix)
iv)
iii)
vi)

iv)–vi) Complete the labels to identify the three seas shown on the map. [3]

vii)–ix) Complete the labels to identify the three cities shown on the map. [3]

6 **a)** Describe the changes made by General Park Chung Hee to improve South Korea's economy.

[4]

b) Name a type of product that South Korea is famous for exporting. [1]

c) What is a chaebol? Give an example of one that manufactures electronic devices.

[2]

7 Outline the political situation of Korea from 1945 onwards.

[4]

Total Marks / 20

Physical Geography

Geological Timescale

1 a) Draw lines to link the rock type to the correct phrase that is associated with it.

Igneous		Formed in layers
Sedimentary		Changed by heat or pressure
Metamorphic		From a volcano

[2]

b) i) What are found in sedimentary rocks and used as evidence to support Darwin's theory of evolution? .... [1]

ii) Study this diagram.

What is the diagram suggesting about evolution?

.... [1]

iii) Describe **two** changes shown in the diagram above.

....

.... [2]

c) Where is sedimentary rock formed?

.... [1]

2 a) State a difference between the first humans that appeared 2.3 million years ago and now.

.... [1]

b) Some movies show humans battling dinosaurs. Why is this **not** correct?

.... [1]

c) Put the following into the correct sequence from newest to oldest:

flowering plants   **dinosaurs**   **jellyfish**   **humans**   **flying insects**

.... [2]

3 **a) i)** Where in the UK are the oldest rocks found?

_____ [1]

ii) Approximately how many years ago were the oldest rocks in the UK formed?

_____ [1]

b) The last time period when parts of the UK were covered in ice was 20 000 years ago.

In which time period was this? _____ [1]

c) What do scientists think caused dinosaurs to become extinct?

_____ [1]

4 The graph below shows global temperature change over a 2000-year period.

a) Add the labels to the graph to show **glacials** and **interglacials**. [1]

b) Describe the relationship between global temperature and sea level change.

_____

_____ [2]

c) Explain why sea levels rise or fall as global temperature changes.

_____

_____ [2]

d) The burning of fossil fuels has caused a lot of greenhouse gases to be released
into the atmosphere. What is this called and what is it contributing to? [2]

_____

_____

_____ [2]

e) What could be a negative impact of sea levels rising and how could this affect people?

_____

_____ [2]

Total Marks _____ / 26

Physical Geography

Plate Tectonics

1 Complete this paragraph using the correct words from the box.

mantle	rim	metal	crust	hot	plates	core

The _____ of the Earth is made of solid _____ . This part of the Earth is

_____ , which causes the _____ to be semi-molten. The Earth's

_____ is made up of several _____ , which move around very slowly.   **[6]**

2 Draw lines to join each plate boundary to the correct description.

Destructive	Plates move towards each other, and an oceanic plate goes underneath a continental plate.
Constructive	Plates slide past each other in opposite directions, or in the same direction at different speeds.
Conservative	Plates move apart from each other and new land or a rift valley is created.

[2]

3 Look at the diagram.

Tick the statements that are correct for this type of plate margin.   **[2]**

Statement	Tick if correct
Pillow lava is formed at the plate margin as lava cools under the sea.	
Plates are moving apart from each other, which causes earthquakes to happen but not volcanoes.	
As magma rises through the plate margin, it cools to form new land and volcanic islands.	
The Great Rift Valley in Africa was formed by this sort of plate boundary on land.	
Land is being destroyed as it melts owing to the magma rising up through the plate margin.	

4 Label the following tectonic plates on the map below.

Eurasian

Nazca

North American

African

South American

A B C D E

[2]

5 Draw lines to join each country to its main type of natural hazard.

Japan	Earthquakes
Iceland	Volcanoes
Tonga	Earthquakes and volcanoes

[2]

6 Each picture below shows the damage caused by a tectonic hazard.

Describe what has happened in each image.

a)

....
....
....
.... [3]

b)

....
....
....
.... [3]

c)

....
....
....
.... [3]

Total Marks .... / 23

Physical Geography

Rocks and Geology

1 The Earth's crust is made up of three types of rock: igneous, sedimentary and metamorphic.

In the rows of the table below, circle the correct answer from the options given for each rock type. **[5]**

	Igneous	Metamorphic	Sedimentary
Where is it formed?	On the seabed / Within the Earth's crust / Where magma cools	On the seabed / Within the Earth's crust / Where magma cools	On the seabed / Within the Earth's crust / Where magma cools
Is it hard or soft?	Hard / Soft	Hard / Soft	Hard / Soft
Is it porous, non-porous or both?	Porous / Non-porous / Both	Porous / Non-porous / Both	Porous / Non-porous / Both
Example	Basalt / Chalk / Marble	Basalt / Chalk / Marble	Basalt / Chalk / Marble
Percentage of the Earth's crust	28% / 65% / 7%	28% / 65% / 7%	28% / 65% / 7%

2 Why are some rocks porous and some non-porous?

....

.... **[2]**

3 Put steps A–E into the correct order to describe the formation of sedimentary rock.

A Material is deposited on the seabed.

B Rock is broken down and removed by weathering and erosion.

C Sediment is compressed as more of it is added on top in layers.

D Material is transported by water to the sea.

E Layered rock is cemented into solid rock.

Correct order: .... **[2]**

4 Why does extrusive igneous rock form quickly?

....

.... **[2]**

5 These images show some metamorphic (A) and sedimentary rock (B).

A   B

Describe why the sedimentary rock will be more easily eroded or weathered than the metamorphic one.

....

....

[2]

6 The diagram shows the rock cycle. Complete the labels for a) to d) using the given terms.

Rising magma in mantle

Sedimentary rock

Heat and pressure

Igneous rock

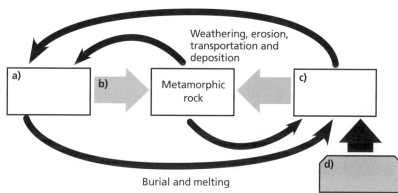

[4]

7 Why could it be said that metamorphic and sedimentary rocks are made from 'second-hand' material?

....

....

[2]

8 Draw lines to join each photograph to the type of rock shown.

A   B   C

| Igneous | Sedimentary | Metamorphic |

[2]

Total Marks .... / 21

Physical Geography

KS3 Geography Workbook

Weathering and Soil

1 Complete the diagram using the options given in the box below.

Biological
Physical
Chemical
Freeze-thaw
Tree/Plant roots
Carbonation
Heating and cooling

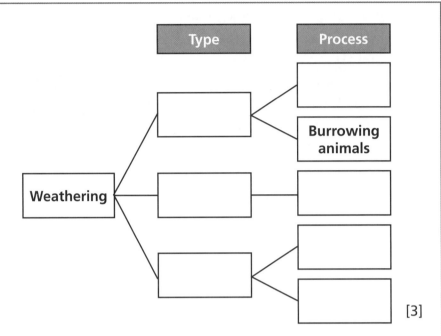

Type   Process

Weathering

Burrowing animals

[3]

2 Write the most likely weathering process that has occurred in each of the pictures below.

a)

b)

c)

[3]

3 For each statement, circle whether it is **true** or **false**.

a) Freeze-thaw weathering only occurs in mountain areas.   **True / False**

b) Biological weathering can affect rock, soil, sand and buildings.   **True / False**

c) Onion-skin weathering only happens if the temperature goes above and below 0°C.   **True / False**

d) Freeze-thaw weathering needs water.   **True / False**

e) Carbonation can affect chalk and limestone cliffs.   **True / False**

f) Heating and cooling only affects softer rocks.   **True / False**   [6]

4 Describe the weathering process shown in this image and how it could affect the cliff over time.

[3]

5 Using data, explain why scientists agree that soil is a **non-renewable** resource.

....

....

.... [3]

6 A diagram of soil horizons (layers) is shown. Use it in parts a) and b) to complete the table.

Horizon	Material	Description
O		
A		
B		
C		
R		

a) Identify each horizon by completing the 'Material' column using these five options:

Topsoil   **Weathered rock fragments**   **Humus**   **Bedrock**   **Subsoil** [2]

b) Now complete the 'Description' column using these five statements.

Parent material: the rock type that the soil is formed of.

Weathered rock is becoming part of the soil.

Surface layer of fallen leaves, animal droppings and insects.

This layer is rich in nutrients, minerals and humus.

Solid rock that is ideal for building foundations to sit on. [2]

7 Explain why soil is so important for life on Earth.

....

....

.... [3]

8 Use the options in the box below to complete the table to show how soil in the UK differs from typical soil found in tropical rainforests. [2]

20–30 m   latosol   2–5 cm   10000 years   20–30 cm   1–2 m   100000000 years   brown earth

	Soil in the UK	Soil in tropical rainforests
Name		
Depth of topsoil		
Overall depth		
Approximate age		

Total Marks .... / 27

Physical Geography

Weather and Climate

1 Describe the difference between **weather** and **climate**.

....

.... [2]

2 Match the weather terms below to the correct symbols in the table.

| Thunderstorms | Hail | Freezing conditions | Gales |
| Snow | Sunny periods | Sunny | Light rain | Heavy rain | [9]

a)	b)	c) ....
d)	e)	f) ....
g)	h)	i) ....

3 Describe what is happening at each of A, B, C and D. Use the words from the box to help you.

| condensation wind |
| heating rises |
| cooler evaporate |

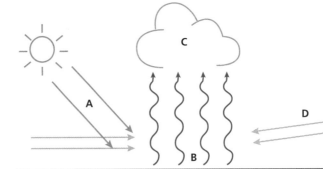

A .... [2]

B .... [2]

C .... [2]

D .... [2]

4 For most people, changes in the weather are just rather inconvenient, but for others they are more important.

Name **three** jobs that depend on having certain weather.

_____ _____ _____ [3]

5 Complete the crossword puzzle.

Across	Down
2. The lowest temperature recorded in a day (7)	**1.** The amount of moisture in the air (8)
5. Hail, sleet, snow and rain are examples of this (13)	**3.** This happens when cold air sinks (4, 8)
6. The highest temperature recorded in a day (7)	**4.** The difference between the lowest and highest daily temperature (5)

[6]

6 The table below shows how different types of weather data is collected using special devices (instruments) and then represented using appropriate units.

Two columns of the table have already been completed. Fill in the rest of the table using the options below.

Knots, mph or m/s   Rain gauge   Anemometer   SE or 135°   25 mph   Barometer

mm   Wind vane   mb   Compass points or degrees   1008 mb   15 mm   [4]

	Rainfall	Temperature	Wind speed	Wind direction	Precipitation type	Pressure
Instrument		Thermometer			Observation	
Unit		°C or °F			Name	
Example		15°C or 60°F			Snow, hail	

Total Marks _____ / 32

Physical Geography

Glaciation

1 Draw lines to join the type of ice to the correct description on the right.

| Ice cap | Forms in valleys high up in mountain ranges called alpine regions. |

| Ice sheet | A large, thick area of ice found on land or sea in the polar regions. |

| Glacier | Found around the edges of the polar regions, these are thinner areas of ice. | [2]

2 Describe the process of the formation of a glacier using the terms below.

> snow   firn   a long period of time   compress   ice   gravity   dense   accumulation

....

....

....

.... [3]

3 Complete the sentences below with appropriate geographical words.

a) Snow and ice changes to water or water vapour as the temperature increases.

This is called .... or .... [2]

b) If accumulation is slow, the glacier appears to move back up the valley.

This is called .... [1]

c) The part of the glacier that is right at the front is called the .... [1]

4 Ice in a glacier is a powerful agent of erosion. There are two main types of glacial erosion called **plucking** and **abrasion**. These happen where the ice is in contact with rock.

Complete the cross-section (X–Y) sketch of the corrie starting to form in the photograph using the labels in the box.

> Steep back wall   Plucking   Abrasion   Corrie   Snow
> Freeze-thaw weathering   Direction of flow   Lip

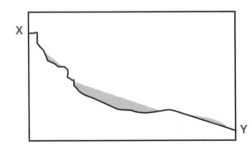

[8]

5 Identify each type of moraine shown in the pictures as either **lateral**, **medial** or **terminal**.

a) _____.

b) _____.

c) _____.

[3]

6 Describe the formation of an erratic like the one shown in the photograph.

_____

_____

_____

_____ [4]

7 Describe why glacial landscapes are popular with visitors. Use examples of specific places.

_____

_____

_____

_____ [4]

8 The photograph shows a queue of hikers at the summit of Snowdon, in the Snowdonia National Park in Wales. This photograph suggests that there may be some problems linked to large numbers of people visiting glaciated landscapes.

Describe **one problem** and **one benefit** to the local area and its residents.

Problem: _____

_____

Benefit: _____

_____ [4]

Total Marks _____ / 32

Physical Geography

Rivers and Coasts

1 Write a suitable label for each numbered feature.

[7]

1	
2	
3	
4	
5	
6	
7	

2 Order the four processes of erosion and transport so that the ones requiring the most energy are at the head of the arrow and the ones requiring the least energy are at the bottom.

Use each of these eight options once only:

Abrasion **Attrition** **Dissolving** **Hydraulic action**
Saltation **Solution** **Suspension** **Traction**

Erosion				
Most energy ⟵ Least energy				
Transport				

[8]

3 A sketch is being made of the meander shown in the photograph.

a) Add labels to the sketch to describe the formation of the meander. [5]

b) Describe what will eventually happen at the point marked **X** on the sketch.

....

....

.... [3]

4 Write the numbers 1–6 in the boxes to order the process of wave formation.

	The circular motion causes small waves that move forward in the direction of the wind.
	The Sun's energy causes variation in air temperature, which causes wind as warm air rises and cooler air fills its place.
	The friction causes a circular motion to start in the water.
	The top of the wave moves faster than the bottom, causing the wave to break.
	When the wave reaches the coast, the friction of the sea floor causes the wave to increase in height.
	The wind blows over the surface of the sea, which causes friction.

[3]

5 Explain, with examples, how each of the following factors can affect coastal erosion.

a) Hard/Soft rock

[3]

b) Fetch

[3]

c) Wave type (constructive/destructive)

[3]

6 With the help of a labelled diagram, explain the formation of caves, arches, stacks and stumps.

[8]

Total Marks _____ / 43

Physical Geography

Landscapes

1 Give a benefit and a drawback for each one of these ways that humans use the Earth's resources. [8]

Use	Benefit	Drawback
Removal of trees to make space for human activity		
Extracting minerals and rocks from mines and quarries		
Extracting water from rivers and underground stores		
Using fossil fuels to provide energy		

2 Explain the term **carrying capacity**, giving an example of somewhere with a low carrying capacity.

....

.... [2]

3 Satellite images are used by governments to protect rainforests from illegal logging.

Why would a country like Brazil need to use a technique like satellite imagery?

....

.... [2]

4 Some companies claim to be 'carbon neutral'.

Which of the following statements are **true**? [2]

Statement	Tick if correct
Carbon-neutral companies do not produce any carbon at all.	
Carbon-neutral companies use strategies to reduce their carbon emissions.	
Trees may be planted to absorb carbon dioxide to offset a company's carbon emissions.	
Carbon-neutral companies always put profit before the environment.	
Some people think some carbon-neutral companies are not telling the truth.	

5 There are several ways to try to reduce damage to fragile environments.
   Look at photographs A and B. Which one of these shows a more sustainable strategy?
   Explain why.   A

   More sustainable: ....

   Explanation: ....

   .... [3]

6 Look at the following images, which show indigenous people.
   Describe what each image shows and give a benefit and a drawback for the people shown.

   a) Maasai people in Kenya   [4]

   Description:...

   ....

   ....

   Benefit: ....

   ....

   Drawback: ....

   ....

   b) A Makoro logboat poler in Botswana (eco-tourism)   [4]

   Description:...

   ....

   ....

   Benefit: ....

   ....

   Drawback: ....

   ....

   Total Marks .... / 25

Human Geography

Population

1 Study the graph below. Tick the correct statements in the table that follows. [2]

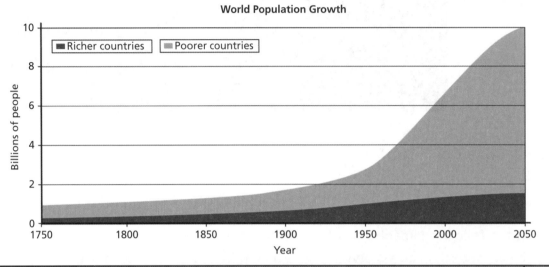

World Population Growth

Statement	Tick if correct
Between 1750 and 1950, the world population grew very rapidly.	
Since 1950, the world population has grown very rapidly.	
By 2050, the world population will be more than 15 billion people.	
The population has grown faster in the poorer countries than the richer countries.	
Since 2000, the world population has started to decrease.	
The world population in 2020 was approximately 7.9 billion people.	
By 2050, there will be more people living in richer countries than in poorer countries.	
World population grew faster from 1950–2000 than from 1850–1900.	

2 Study the map.
Identify:

a) two countries that are densely populated

....

.... [2]

b) two countries that are sparsely populated

....

.... [2]

· One dot represents 100 000 people

3 Define the term **population density**.

.... [1]

4 Using examples, explain why some parts of the world are very densely populated.

....

....

....

....
[4]

5 Match each description on the left to the most suitable term on the right. [3]

The process of people moving into a country	International migration
People who move to a country for jobs and higher wages	Emigration
People fleeing conflict or persecution	Immigration
	Economic migrants
	Asylum seekers
	Refugees

6 Give **two** reasons why birth rates in some low income countries are high.

....

....
[2]

7 Complete the table below to show **two** advantages and **two** disadvantages of an ageing population. [4]

Advantages	Disadvantages

Total Marks .... / 20

Human Geography

Urbanisation

1 Write the key terms below next to the correct definition in the table.

Urbanisation   Suburbanisation   Counterurbanisation

Key term	Definition
	People move from cities to surrounding smaller towns and villages
	Increasing proportions of people living in towns and cities
	People moving outwards within a city, causing the city to grow

[2]

2 Use the information below to draw a line graph showing how the population of Nairobi in Kenya has changed through time.

Population of Nairobi in Kenya	
Year	Population
1980	860 000
1990	1 380 000
2000	2 210 000
2010	3 230 000
2020	4 730 000

[2]

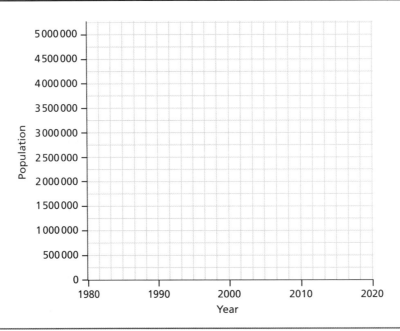

3 Define the term **megacity**.

.... [1]

4 Explain why many cities in lower income countries are growing rapidly.

....

....

....

.... [4]

5 a) Many people in cities like Nairobi in Kenya end up living in shanty towns. Write three
labels around the picture below showing some of the features of shanty towns. [3]

b) Choose **one** of the features you identified in part a) and explain how it would affect
people's quality of life.

Feature ....

Effect on people's quality of life ....

....

.... [2]

6 Complete the table below. Identify **one** way in which housing, transport and waste in cities
in high income countries can be made more sustainable.

Feature of city	How it can be made more sustainable
Housing	
Transport	
Waste	

[3]

Total Marks .... / 17

Human Geography

Development

1 Write the correct key terms in the table from the choices given.

Birth rate   **Death rate**   **Life expectancy**
Adult literacy   **Gross domestic product**   **Infant mortality**

Key term	Definition
	The number of children that die before they reach their first birthday per 1000 live births per year
	The total value of goods and services produced by a country per year
	The percentage of people over 15 that can read and write

[3]

2 Define the term **development**.

[1]

3 Outline **one** disadvantage of using a single measure of development, such as gross domestic product.

[2]

4 Study the map.

Human Development Index, 2017

The Human Development Index (HDI) is a summary measure of key dimensions of human development: a long and healthy life, a good education, and having a decent standard of living.

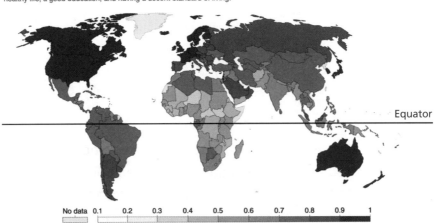

No data 0.1 0.2 0.3 0.4 0.5 0.6 0.7 0.8 0.9 1

Describe the distribution of countries that score between 0.9 and 1 on the Human Development Index.

[2]

5 Explain why some countries are slow to develop.

....

....

....

....

[4]

6 This information shows where the money goes from the sale of a bag of Fair Trade coffee.

Grower 25%	Country of coffee growth
Transport 7%	Transport company
Roasting and bagging 8%	Country of coffee company head office
Labels and bags 5%	
Coffee company expenses 30%	
Supermarket that sells the coffee 25%	

Complete the table to show where the money paid by a customer for a bag of coffee goes.

Where the money goes	Percentage
Country of coffee growth	
Transport company	7
Country of coffee company head office	

[2]

7 Which of the statements best describes Fair Trade? Tick the correct answer in the table below.

Statement	Tick if correct
Producers receive a price that gives a reasonable profit.	
Producers get paid the lowest price possible.	
Producers sell their products at a cheap price.	

[1]

8 Complete the table below to show **two** advantages and **two** disadvantages of aid.

Advantages	Disadvantages

[4]

Total Marks .... / 19

Human Geography

1 Put the following jobs into the correct column of the table according to their economic activity classification.

Nurse   Farmer   Accountant   Baker   IT consultant   Builder

Primary	Secondary	Tertiary	Quaternary

[4]

2 Use the information in the table to complete the pie chart showing the UK's employment structure.

Economic activity	Percentage employed
Primary	1
Secondary	18
Tertiary and Quaternary	81

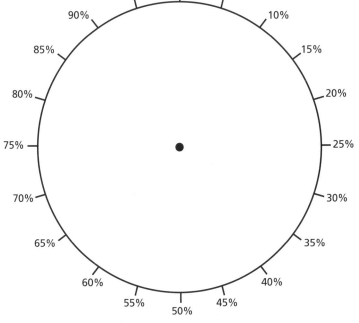

[2]

3 Give **one** way in which the employment structure of a lower income country, such as Kenya, might be different to a high income country, such as the UK.

....

.... [1]

4 Explain why the UK imports food.

....

....

....

....

.... [4]

5 Define the term **organic farming**.

.... [1]

6 Use the terms below to complete the following paragraph.

| LICs | HICs | NICs | higher | less | more | lower |

Manufacturing mainly used to take place in ...., such as the UK and USA.

A lot of manufacturing now occurs in .... and ...., such as China,

Brazil and Mexico. In these countries, labour costs are ...., land is often

cheaper and environmental laws are .... strict. [5]

7 Look at the illustration below, which shows some placards held by people at a protest. Give **two** reasons why these people might be protesting.

.... [2]

8 Which of the statements in the table below correctly describe work in the tertiary and quaternary sectors? Tick the **two** correct answers.

Statement	Tick if correct
Tertiary and quaternary sector jobs are the main type of job in HICs.	
All tertiary and quaternary sector jobs are very highly paid.	
In HICs, the number of people working in the tertiary and quaternary sectors has decreased over time.	
There are a wide range of different types of tertiary and quaternary jobs.	

[2]

Total Marks .... / 21

Human Geography

Natural Resources

1 Put the following resources into the correct column of the table according to their resource type.

Oil   Solar energy   Wood   Iron ore

Non-renewable	Renewable

[2]

2 Define the term **sustainable**.

.... [1]

3 Explain **two** ways by which non-renewable resources can be made to last longer.

....

....

....

.... [2]

4 Complete the table to show **two** advantages and **two** disadvantages of chopping down forests.

Advantages	Disadvantages

[4]

5 Complete the following sentences to define each term.

Overfishing is ....

....

Fish farms are ....

.... [2]

6 The charts below show how the types of fuel to create electricity in the UK have changed over time.

Which of the statements in the table below correctly describe the changes that have taken place? Tick the correct answers.

UK Energy Generation by Fuel Type

2000

Hydro 1.4%
Nuclear 22.6%
Coal 31.8%
Gas 39.3%
Oil 3.6%

2020

Other Renewables 12.6%
Oil 3.3%
Gas 35.7%
Wind and Solar 28.4%
Hydro 2.2%
Nuclear 16.1%

Statement	Tick if correct
Gas is the main type of fuel used to create electricity.	
Nuclear was used more than wind and solar in 2020 to create electricity.	
In 2020, oil was the most used fuel to create electricity.	
Between 2000 and 2020, the amount of electricity created by hydro doubled.	
The amount of coal used to create electricity rapidly decreased from 2000 to 2020.	
Renewable energy as a source of electricity increased between 2000 and 2020.	

[2]

7 Explain why the types of energy being used in the UK are changing over time.

....

....

....

....

[4]

Total Marks .... / 17

Geography Skills

Ordnance Survey Maps

Look at the Ordnance Survey map, which shows part of North Norfolk, and answer the following questions. The scale is 1 : 50 000

one grid square is 1 km

N

1 List **five** pieces of evidence from the map that show Hunstanton is popular with tourists.

[5]

2 What direction is Holme next the Sea from Hunstanton? [1]

3 What direction is Ringstead from Thornham? [1]

4 What is the name of the park in grid square 6941? [1]

5 Give a four-figure grid reference for the centre of Ringstead. [1]

6 What is the name of the farm in grid square 7041? [1]

7 Give a six-figure grid reference for the golf course south of Hunstanton. [1]

8 What is at 742405? [1]

9 Give a six-figure grid reference for Gore Point (north of Holme next the Sea). [1]

10 Describe the relief of the land in this area of North Norfolk.

[2]

11 What height does the land reach in grid square 7241? m [1]

12 What are the intervals between the contour lines on this map? m [1]

13 What is the width of the beach next to the Sea Life Sanctuary in Hunstanton? m [1]

14 Estimate the distance between the villages of Ringstead and Sedgeford. km [1]

15 Estimate the distance from the car park in Old Hunstanton to the Holme Dunes National Nature Reserve along the Peddars Way and Norfolk Coast path. km [1]

Total Marks / 20

Geography Skills

Geographic Information Systems

1 Which of the statements below correctly describe Geographic Information Systems? Tick the correct answers.

Statement	Tick if correct
Geographic Information Systems are online textbooks providing descriptions and explanations of key geographical concepts.	
Computer hardware, software and digital data is used to create maps.	
Data can be changed, analysed and viewed in different ways to see geographical patterns and relationships.	
Data is sorted out so it can be displayed using various graphical techniques.	
Maps are drawn by hand to show the layout of places.	
Geographic Information Systems can be accessed using a computer or a tablet.	
Geographic Information Systems use layers of information stacked on top of each other.	
Spreadsheets are a good example of Geographic Information Systems.	

[2]

2 Give **two** examples of organisations/businesses that use Geographic Information Systems (GIS) and explain why they use them.

Name of organisation/business ....

Why they use GIS ....

....

Name of organisation/business ....

Why they use GIS ....

[4]

....

3 How is relief shown on a map?

....

....

[2]

4 The features on a digital map are divided into four types.

Draw a line between each feature type to match it to its definition. [2]

Points	Symbols that show things such as rivers and roads
Lines	Used for the names of places or landscape features
Polygons	Symbols that represent a feature at a particular location
Text	Shapes to show things such as buildings, lakes and forests

5 Define the term **geotechnologies**.

.... [1]

6 What is Google Earth?

....

.... [2]

7 Images A and B below show parts of the Amazon rainforest in South America.

Label the one which is an aerial photograph and the one which is a satellite image. [1]

A

B

....

8 One of the features of Google Earth is a timeline that shows how an area has changed over time.

Explain why this might be useful when studying tropical rainforests.

....

.... [1]

Total Marks .... / 15

Geography Skills

Fieldwork

1 Complete the table below by putting the stages of a geography fieldwork investigation in order.

Stage of geography fieldwork	Rank order (1 = first, 6 = last)
Collecting data	
Displaying data	
Setting a question/hypothesis	
Drawing conclusions	
Collating data	
Analysing data	

[2]

2 **a)** Look at the diagram below. Tick the correct box to identify the type of sampling shown.

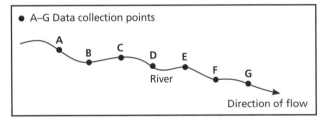

• A–G Data collection points

River

Direction of flow

Type of sampling	Tick if correct
Random	
Stratified	
Systematic	
Opportunity sampling	

[1]

b) Suggest why the type of sampling shown in the diagram above is not always possible in a fieldwork enquiry.

_____

_____

[2]

3 The questionnaire below was used to find out how far people travelled to a seaside resort and how long they stayed there. 20 people were asked.

Visitor Questionnaire	
1	How old are you?
2	Where have you come from?
3	What method of transport did you use to get here?
4	Have you visited here before?

Suggest **two** ways the questionnaire could be improved to make it more useful.

_____

_____

[2]

4 The table below shows how the width of a river changes with distance downstream.

Location	A	B	C	D	E	F	G
Distance downstream (m)	500	1000	1500	2000	2500	3000	3500
River width (m)	1.5	1.8	2.2	2.5	3.1	2.8	3.8

a) Suggest a suitable method for presenting the data shown.

.... [1]

b) Apart from river width, suggest another type of data that could be collected along the course of a river.

.... [1]

c) Outline the conclusions that could be drawn from the data above.

....

....

.... [2]

5 a) Complete the chart below by adding the following information. [2]

Type of transport	Percentage of visitors
Bus	5
Car	55

Key

🚲 Bicycle

🚂 Train

🚌 Bus

🚗 Car

One symbol represents 10%

b) Suggest another way of presenting this data.

.... [1]

c) Explain why the method you identified in part b) is a suitable method.

.... [1]

d) Outline the main conclusion that could be drawn from the data above.

.... [1]

Total Marks .... / 16

1 Study the diagram below.

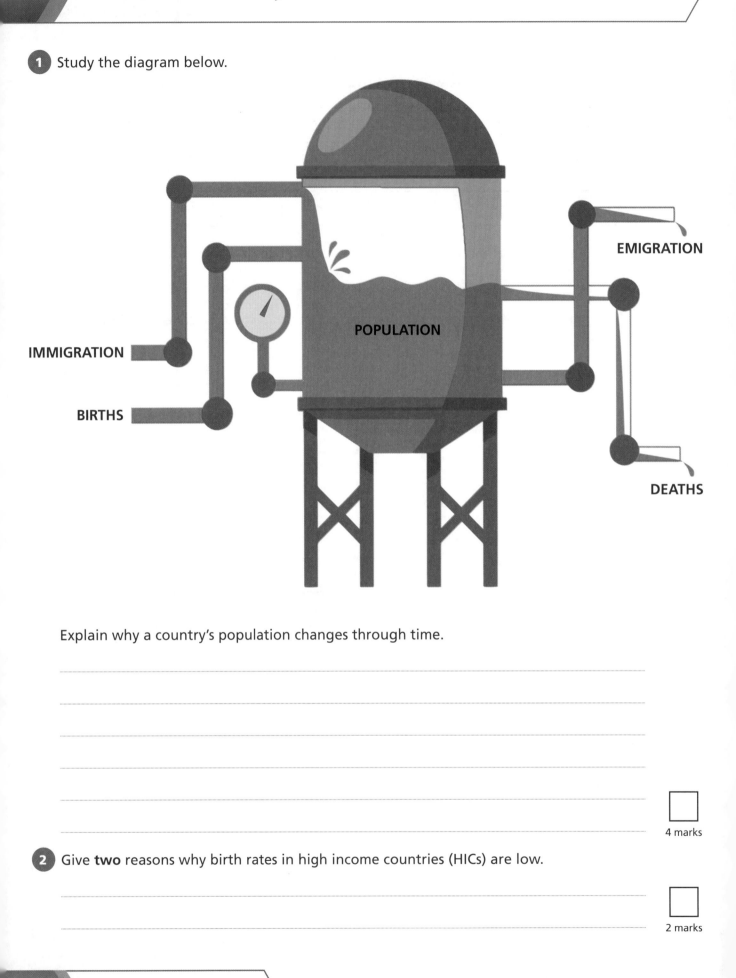

EMIGRATION

POPULATION

IMMIGRATION

BIRTHS

DEATHS

Explain why a country's population changes through time.

....

....

....

....

....

....

4 marks

2 Give **two** reasons why birth rates in high income countries (HICs) are low.

....

....

2 marks

3 **a)** In which **two** continents does Russia have shared borders?

2 marks

b) Name **four** countries that Russia shares a land border with.

4 marks

4 Why did China introduce the One Child Policy in 1979?

2 marks

5 **a)** In what year is India's population predicted to overtake China's?

1 mark

b) How many people are expected to live in India when that happens?

1 mark

6 Tick the statements that are **true**.

Statement	Tick if correct
Scientists can accurately predict when volcanoes are going to erupt and usually evacuate people to safety.	
Volcanoes cause fires but earthquakes do not.	
It is easy to protect people and buildings from the hot lava and ash from a volcanic eruption.	
It is almost impossible to predict exactly when an earthquake will happen.	
Land is being destroyed as it melts owing to the magma rising up through the plate margin.	

2 marks

7 Look at this photograph of a village in the UK.

List **two** reasons why people would be attracted to live here.

....

....

2 marks

8 Describe the effects of counterurbanisation on rural areas.

....

....

....

....

4 marks

9 Describe how satellites are used in weather forecasts.

....

....

....

....

3 marks

10 a) Explain why the Suez Canal is such an important waterway economically for global shipping.

....
....
....
....

3 marks

b) Describe an environmental benefit of the Suez Canal.

....
....
....

2 marks

11 Describe the type of farming shown in the photograph.

....
....

2 marks

Mixed Test-Style Questions

12 Complete the table below by giving one named example of a HIC, NIC and LIC.

Type of country	Named example
High income country (HIC)	
Newly industrialising country (NIC)	
Low income country (LIC)	

3 marks

13 Explain what is meant by the Human Development Index.

....

....

....

3 marks

14 Which of the statements below correctly describe economic activity in the UK?

Tick the correct answers.

Statement	Tick if correct
As the standard of living in the UK has increased, more people have been employed in secondary activities.	
Over 70% of people work in the tertiary and quaternary sectors.	
The number of people employed in primary activities has decreased due to the population of the UK falling.	
Machines do a lot of the work in primary and secondary activities, meaning that fewer people work in these types of jobs.	

2 marks

15 Describe what is meant by **indigenous people** and give an example.

....

....

....

....

3 marks

16 Explain why the traditional way of life of indigenous people is under threat in some areas.

....

....

....

....

☐ 3 marks

17 Explain why South Korea's economy grew between 1953 and 1987, when the GDP increased from $872 to $7455.

....

....

....

....

☐ 3 marks

18 Order the time periods from the longest to the shortest. Give **one** example of each.

Periods   Eons   Eras

Ordered longest to shortest: ....

Example of a Period: ....

Example of an Eon: ....

Example of an Era: ....

☐ 4 marks

19 In 2022, there was a record-breaking heatwave in the UK during which temperatures of over 40°C were recorded. A devastating monsoon resulted in one-third of Bangladesh being under water, killing more than 1000 people.

Why do some scientists think these extreme events are becoming more common?

....

....

....

....

☐ 3 marks

20 Explain why a large amount of manufacturing now takes place in newly industrialising countries such as China.

....

....

....

....

4 marks

21 Look at the photograph below.

Complete the following sentences by circling the correct option in each pair.

The tree in the photograph is **deciduous / coniferous**.

These types of trees are **softwood / hardwood**.

An example of this type of tree is **oak / pine**.

These trees are **slow growing / fast growing**.

4 marks

22 The photographs below show three ways that humans can get income from living near to volcanoes.

State what each activity is and say whether it is primary, secondary or tertiary.

a)

Activity: ....

....

Primary, secondary or tertiary?

....

b)

Activity: ....

....

Primary, secondary or tertiary?

....

c)

Activity: ....

....

Primary, secondary or tertiary?

....

6 marks

23 Explain why the UK imports gas from countries such as Norway and Qatar.

....

....

....

....

3 marks

Mixed Test-Style Questions

24 List **two** ways in which the relief of the land is shown on an Ordnance Survey map.

....

....

2 marks

25 Use the correct words from the box below to complete the following paragraph.

patterns	census	computer	General	Geographic
	presented	layers	erased	

GIS stands for .... Information System. This involves using

.... of information so that data can be .... and

analysed for different locations. This enables .... and relationships to

be identified.

4 marks

26 Explain why a delivery company might use a Geographic Information System.

....

....

....

2 marks

27 This picture shows metamorphic rock.

a) Describe how it formed.

....

....

....

....

....

5 marks

b) This is a picture of slate used on a roof. Why is it good to use for roof tiles?

☐ 4 marks

28 Explain **one** reason why volcanoes might be important to a country and its people.

☐ 3 marks

29 For each pair below, describe **one** difference between them.

a) Oceanic crust / Continental crust

☐ 1 mark

b) Earth's inner core / Mantle

☐ 1 mark

c) Destructive plate margin / Constructive plate margin

☐ 1 mark

d) Focus / Epicentre (of an earthquake)

☐ 1 mark

e) Shield volcano / Composite volcano

☐ 1 mark

f) Active volcano / Dormant volcano

☐ 1 mark

Mixed Test-Style Questions

30 Complete the table to show **one** advantage and **one** disadvantage of using closed questions in a questionnaire. Then give **one** advantage and **one** disadvantage of using open questions.

	Closed question	Open question
Advantage		
Disadvantage		

4 marks

31 List **two** types of data that could be collected in an urban area.

....

....

2 marks

32 The photograph shows part of a cliff that has collapsed onto the beach below.

Describe how this has happened through physical weathering.

....

....

....

....

....

4 marks

33 Why is exfoliation also called onion-skin weathering?

....

....

....

3 marks

34 Describe **two** ways that these creatures weather the rock they live on.

....

....

2 marks

35 a) Draw lines to match each label to the appropriate climate graph.

Desert   **Monsoon**   **Savannah**   **Equatorial**

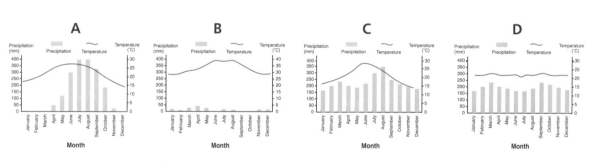

2 marks

b) Draw lines to match each label to the appropriate climate graph.

Steppe   **Tundra**   **Polar**   **Mediterranean**

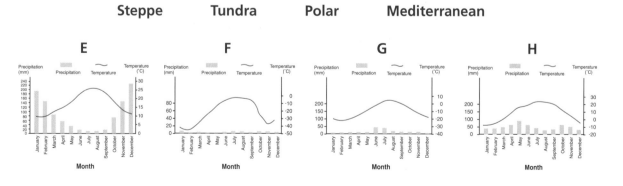

2 marks

36 Study the Ordnance Survey map of part of Snowdonia National Park in Wales, and the photograph that follows. The scale of the map is 1 : 25 000

one grid square is 1 km

N

a) This photograph was taken at 705131. Which direction was the photographer facing?

1 mark

b) What is the name of the lake in the photograph?

1 mark

c) How far away is the lake from the photographer? _____ m

☐ 1 mark

d) Is there a footpath around the lake? _____

☐ 1 mark

e) i) What type of glacial landform is the lake part of? _____

☐ 1 mark

ii) What information does the map give to help you come to this conclusion?

_____

_____

_____

☐ 3 marks

f) Give a six-figure grid reference for the centre of Llyn Cau. _____

☐ 1 mark

g) What is the highest point on the map? _____ m

☐ 1 mark

37 Sort the following terms into the appropriate environment column of the table.

Traction   Hydraulic action   Stump   Meander   Meltwater Floodplain   Longshore drift   Moraine   Suspension Slip-off slope (point – bar)   Steep back wall   Fetch   Plucking   Lip

Terms can be used more than once and each box of the table should have a term in it.

Coasts	Fluvial	Glacial

☐ 3 marks

Mixed Test-Style Questions

38 a) A teacher is using a torch and a globe to explain to the class why it is colder at the Equator than at the two poles.

How does this help the teacher to explain this to them?

_____

_____

_____

_____

4 marks

b) Corries and glaciers form in north-facing valleys in the Northern Hemisphere and in south-facing valleys in the Southern Hemisphere.

Explain why this is the case by labelling the diagram of a post-glacial landscape below. Use the following words to help you describe the features:

aspect   north   south   shadow   accumulate   snow   melt

A tarn in a corrie in the Northern Hemisphere

6 marks

c) There are still alpine glaciers that can form on mountainsides that face the sun. Why is this?

_____

_____

2 marks

39 a) A teacher asks their class the following question: "Which of the four processes of erosion is **not** responsible for the formation of landforms and why?"

Write down your answer to this question.

....

....

....

2 marks

b) A student puts up their hand and says that they think there are exceptional cases where the process identified in part a) does indeed create landforms, such as the profile and slope angles of a beach. The student uses the photographs below to support their argument.

Why might the student have a valid point?

....

....

....

2 marks

40 Students have collected fieldwork data about the number of tourists visiting different parts (A, B, C, D and E) of their local town. They have used the data to create this map.

Pedestrian Density Map
(Number of people per hour)

Key:

- 0–20
- 21–40
- 41–60
- 60+

a) What type of map have the students chosen to represent the data?

....

1 mark

b) i) Which area of town received the fewest tourists?

....

1 mark

ii) Why can't we tell exactly how many people visited this area?

....

1 mark

Mixed Test-Style Questions

41 A travel agent is offering trips to Kenya, which give tourists time both on safari and at a beach resort. Complete the speech bubbles below with **one** point each to show how the people pictured may feel about this offer.

Maasai people

One of the benefits could be…

One of the drawbacks could be…

A hotel manager in Mombasa

One of the benefits could be…

One of the drawbacks could be…

An environmentalist

One of the benefits could be…

One of the drawbacks could be…

6 marks

42 Explain why a local resident in a town with a river that regularly floods might disagree with environmentalists over whether hard or soft engineering techniques should be used. Consider both sets of views in your answer.

4 marks

Total Marks _____ / 160

Answers

Page 148: Location Knowledge – Russia

1. a) i) Barents Sea [1]
    ii) Kara Sea [1]
    iii) East Siberian Sea [1]
    iv) Bering Sea [1]
    v) Sea of Okhotsk [1]
    vi) St Petersburg [1]
    vii) Moscow [1]
    viii) Yekaterinburg [1]
    ix) Novosibirsk [1]
    b) Lake Baikal [1]
2. a) **Any one from:** Coal; oil; natural gas [1]
    b) Gold [1]
    c) Timber [1]
    d) $30 trillion [1]
3. a) **Any two suitable points, e.g.** The Steppe region consists of grassland [1] plains. It is a dry region [1] and forests cannot grow there [1]. The soil is call chernozem [1].
    b) **Any two suitable points, e.g.** The land is very fertile [1] and is good for growing crops [1] and raising animals [1]. It provides food for Russia [1] and also for export [1] to other countries.

Page 149: Location Knowledge – China

4. a) i) Russia [1]
    ii) North Korea [1]
    iii) Japan [1]
    iv) India [1]
    v) Thailand [1]
    vi) Xi'an [1]
    vii) Shanghai [1]
    viii) Wuhan [1]
    ix) Shenzen [1]
    b) Gobi [1]; Taklamakan [1]
5. **Any three suitable points, e.g.** It was relaxed/changed [1] from 2015 to allow two children per family [1]. It changed again to allow three children per family [1].
6. **Any two suitable points, e.g.** It holds 3000 types of plants [1] and 4700 types of animals [1]. Rainforests are important in protecting the planet from global warming [1].
7. **Any two suitable points, e.g.** The communist system [1] means that the government controls industry and agriculture [1].

Page 150: Location Knowledge – India

1. a) i) Pakistan [1]
    ii) Nepal [1]
    iii) Bangladesh [1]
    iv) Sri Lanka [1]
    v) New Delhi [1]
    vi) Jaipur [1]
    vii) Lucknow [1]
    viii) Bengaluru (Bangalore) [1]
    b) Himalayas [1]
    c) Arabian Sea [1]; Bay of Bengal [1]
2. a) **Any one from:** tea; coffee [1]
    b) **Any two secondary industries, e.g.** motor vehicles [1]; shipbuilding [1]; computers [1]; textiles [1]; chemicals [1]
    Any two tertiary industries, e.g. telecommunications [1]; software development [1]; pharmaceuticals [1]
3. **Any suitable description that includes these points:**
    Winter: December to March [1]
    Summer (dry): April to June [1]
    Monsoon (rainy): July to September [1]
    Autumn: October to November [1]

Page 151: Location Knowledge – The Middle East

4. i) Turkey [1]
    ii) Egypt [1]
    iii) Iran [1]
    iv) Saudi Arabia [1]
    v) Yemen [1]
    vi) Mediterranean Sea [1]
    vii) Caspian Sea [1]
    viii) Red Sea [1]
    ix) Arabian Sea [1]
    x) Tehran [1]
    xi) Cairo [1]
    xii) Riyadh [1]
    xiii) Muscat [1]
5. Mediterranean [1]; hot desert [1]
6. Oil [1]
7. a) Lowest GDP is Yemen [1] ($690 per capita) and the highest is Qatar [1] ($61 276 per capita).
    b) Approximately $3.6 trillion in 2021 [1]

Page 152: Location Knowledge – Kenya

1. i) South Sudan [1] ii) Ethiopia [1] iii) Somalia [1]
    iv) Uganda [1] v) Tanzania [1] vi) Lake Turkana [1]
    vii) Lake Victoria [1]   viii) Indian Ocean [1]
    ix) Nairobi [1] x) Mombasa [1]

2. **Any four suitable points, e.g.** One of Kenya's main exports is tea [1]; 35 million kg [1] is produced annually. Flowers [1] are another major export, with 35 000 tonnes [1] annually, many end up in UK supermarkets [1]. Other exports include coffee [1] and vegetables [1].

3. A tribe of nomadic pastoralists [1] in Kenya.

4. **Any four suitable points, e.g.** Kenya has a warm/hot climate [1]. People travel to enjoy the beaches [1] and coral reefs [1]. Many tourists enjoy going on safari [1] as Kenya has huge numbers of wild animals [1].

Page 153: Location Knowledge – South Korea

5. i) China [1] ii) North Korea [1] iii) Japan [1] iv) Yellow Sea [1] v) Sea of Japan [1] vi) East China Sea [1] vii) Incheon [1] viii) Seoul [1] ix) Busan [1]

6. a) **Any four suitable points, e.g.** He built new roads [1] to improve communications [1]. Factories were put under government control [1]. Manufacturing [1] was made a priority, for example shipbuilding / vehicle production / textiles / electronic goods [1]. New schools were built [1] to improve education [1].

   b) **Any one from:** electronics; vehicles [1]

   c) Chaebols are South Korea's large companies [1], e.g. Samsung; LG [1]

7. **Any four suitable points, e.g.** Japan controlled Korea [1] until 1945 when it was liberated by Soviet [1] and American [1] forces. The country split in two [1]. Civil war between North and South Korea ran from 1950 to 1953 [1] and 3 000 000 people were killed [1]. A new leader took over in South Korea in 1953 [1] and then in 1987 there were the first free elections [1].

Pages 154–169 Physical Geography

Pages 154–155: Geological Timescale

1. a) **Boxes joined as follows:**

   Igneous – From a volcano
   Sedimentary – Formed in layers
   Metamorphic – Changed by heat or pressure
   [2 marks for all correct; 1 mark if one error]

   b) i) Fossils [1]

   ii) **Any suitable point, e.g.** That species/creatures/animals can change/adapt over time [1]; that evolution can take millions of years [1].

   iii) **Any two suitable points, e.g.** The fish's fins have evolved/changed into legs [1]. The tail has become longer and thinner [1]. The creature has changed to breathe in the air rather than under water [1]. The creature's eyes have moved from being at the side of the head to closer to the top [1].

   c) On the seabed / ocean floor [1]

2. a) **Any suitable point, e.g.** Humans stand more upright than they used to [1]. Humans' brains have increased in size [1]. Humans have less body hair than they used to have [1].

   b) **Any suitable point, e.g.** Dinosaurs were on Earth a long time before humans [1]. Dinosaurs were extinct / wiped out long before humans existed [1].

   c) Jellyfish, flying insects, dinosaurs, flowering plants, humans **[2] [1 mark if one error]**

3. a) i) **Any one from:** North-west Scotland; North Wales [1]

   ii) 2500–3000 million years ago [1]

   b) Quaternary period [1]

   c) An asteroid striking the Earth (accept 'volcanic activity') [1]

4. a) Red peaks labelled as interglacials; blue peaks labelled as glacials [1]

   b) Global temperature increase leads to a rise in sea levels [1]. Global temperature decrease leads to a fall in sea levels. [1]

   c) **Any two suitable points, e.g.** As temperature decreases, more water is locked up [1] in ice caps and ice sheets [1]. When global temperatures increase, ice sheets and ice caps melt [1], meaning that more water is in the oceans [1].

   d) It is called the enhanced greenhouse effect [1] and it is contributing to global warming [1].

   e) **Any suitable points that are linked, e.g.** Greater risk of flooding of (low lying) areas [1] and people could lose their homes [1].

Pages 156–157: Plate Tectonics

1. The **core** of the Earth is made of solid **metal**. This part of the Earth is **hot**, which causes the **mantle** to be semi-molten. The Earth's **crust** is made up of several **plates**, which move around very slowly. **[1 mark each]**

2. **Boxes joined as follows:**
   Destructive – Plates move towards each other, and an oceanic plate goes underneath a continental plate.
   Constructive – Plates move apart from each other and new land or a rift valley is created.
   Conservative – Plates slide past each other in opposite directions, or in the same direction at different speeds.
   [2 marks if all correct; 1 mark if one error only]

3. **These statements should be ticked:**
   Pillow lava is formed at the plate margin as lava cools under the sea.
   As magma rises through the plate margin, it cools to form new land and volcanic islands.
   The Great Rift Valley in Africa was formed by this sort of plate boundary on land.
   [2 marks if all correct; 1 mark if one error only]

4. A – North American; B – Eurasian; C – African; D – South American; E – Nazca

[2 marks if all correct; 1 mark if one error only]

5. **Boxes joined as follows:**

Japan – Earthquakes

Iceland – Earthquakes and volcanoes

Tonga – Volcanoes

[2 marks if all correct; 1 mark if one error only]

6. a) A volcano has erupted **[1]** and lava has flowed from it **[1]** and has cooled to form new rock **[1]**.

b) An earthquake has occurred **[1]** and the shaking ground **[1]** has caused a road bridge to collapse **[1]**.

c) A tsunami has occurred **[1]**, where a large wave (caused by an earthquake/volcano) **[1]** has carried a boat inland **[1]**.

Pages 158–159: Rocks and Geology

1. **Options should be circled to match the answers below.**

	Igneous	Metamorphic	Sedimentary
Where is it formed?	Where magma cools	Within the Earth's crust	On the seabed
Is it hard or soft?	Hard	Hard	Soft
Is it porous, non-porous or both?	Both	Non-porous	Porous
Example	Basalt	Marble	Chalk
Percentage of the Earth's crust	65%	28%	7%

[1 mark for each correct row]

2. **Any two suitable points, e.g.** Rocks are made up of grains **[1]**, which might be tightly packed together (non-porous) **[1]** or the grains might have space between them (porous) **[1]**.

3. Correct order: B, D, A, C, E

[2 marks if all correct; 1 mark if one error only]

4. **Any two suitable points, e.g.** Igneous rock is made from molten rock (magma) **[1]**, which will cool very quickly **[1]** when it comes into contact with air/water **[1]**.

5. **Any two suitable points, e.g.** The sedimentary rock has cracks/gaps/joints/holes **[1]** that mean it could be easily weathered/eroded **[1]** by water/ice/physical weathering **[1]**, carbonation (chemical weathering) **[1]** or plant roots (biological weathering) **[1]**.

6. a) Sedimentary rock **[1]**

b) Heat and pressure **[1]**

c) Igneous rock **[1]**

d) Rising magma in mantle **[1]**

7. **Any two suitable points, e.g.** Metamorphic rock is formed from existing rock that changes **[1]** and sedimentary is made from sediment that includes eroded rock **[1]**. Igneous rock is made from 'new' magma **[1]**.

8. **Images and boxes joined as follows:**

A – Sedimentary; B – Igneous;

C – Metamorphic

[2 marks if all correct; 1 mark if one error only]

Pages 160–161: Weathering and Soil

1.

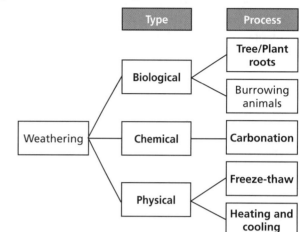

[3 marks if all correct; 2 marks if up to two errors; 1 mark if up to four errors]

2. a) **Any one from:** freeze-thaw; frost shattering **[1]**

b) **Any one from:** onion-skin; heating and cooling; exfoliation **[1]**

c) Carbonation **[1]**

3. a) False **[1]**

b) True **[1]**

c) False **[1]**

d) True **[1]**

e) True **[1]**

f) False **[1]**

4. **Any three suitable points, e.g.** This is an example of biological weathering **[1]**. The bird has burrowed/dug **[1]** into the soft rock/cliff **[1]** to make its nest. Over time, there could be more burrows/nests that weaken the cliff/rock **[1]** and cause it to collapse **[1]**.

5. **Any three suitable points, e.g.** Soil is being lost to soil erosion **[1]** at the rate of 75 billion tonnes a year **[1]**. As it takes a very long time for soil to form **[1]**, for example hundreds of years for 1 cm **[1]**, it is being lost faster than it is being replaced **[1]**.

6. **Table completed as follows:**

Horizon	Material	Description
O	Humus	Surface layer of fallen leaves, animal droppings and insects.
A	Topsoil	This layer is rich in nutrients, minerals and humus.
B	Subsoil	Weathered rock is becoming part of the soil.
C	Weathered rock fragments	Parent material: the rock type that the soil is formed of.
R	Bedrock	Solid rock that is ideal for building foundations to sit on.

a) See 'Material' column above.

[2 marks if all correct; 1 mark if one error only]

b) See 'Description' column above.

[2 marks if all correct; 1 mark if one error only]

7. Any three suitable points, e.g. Soil is where plants grow [1]. Plants provide food for animals and humans [1]. If there was not enough soil, then humans would not have enough food to survive [1]. All living things on land rely on soil for their food [1].

8. Table completed as follows:

	Soil in the UK	Soil in tropical rainforests
Name	Brown earth	Latosol
Depth of topsoil	20–30 cm	2–5 cm
Overall depth	1–2 m	20–30 m
Approximate age	10 000 years	100 000 000 years

[2 marks if fully correct; 1 mark if one error only]

Pages 162–163: Weather and Climate

1. Weather is the day-to-day changes in the atmosphere [1] and climate is the long-term pattern of weather [1].

2. a) Sunny periods [1] b) Light rain [1] c) Sunny [1]
   d) Freezing conditions [1] e) Thunderstorms [1]
   f) Gales [1] g) Heavy rain [1] h) Hail [1] i) Snow [1]

3. Any suitable points up to a maximum of 2 marks for each letter:
   A The Sun's energy [1] is heating the surface of the Earth/ground [1].
   B As the ground is heated the air starts to rise [1] and water at the surface will evaporate [1].
   C The warm air becomes cooler as it rises [1] and condensation occurs [1], forming clouds [1].
   D Cooler air comes in to replace the warm air [1] that has risen, this causes wind [1].

4. Any three suitable answers, e.g. farmer [1]; fisher [1]; owners of hotels / tourist facilities [1]; pilot [1]; ski instructor [1]; delivery driver [1]

5. Across: 2 – minimum [1]; 5 – precipitation [1]; 6 – maximum [1] Down: 1 – humidity [1]; 3 – high pressure [1]; 4 – range [1]

6. Table completed as follows:

	Rainfall	Wind speed	Wind direction	Pressure
Instrument	Rain gauge	Anemometer	Wind vane	Barometer
Unit	mm	Knots, mph or m/s	Compass points or degrees	mb
Example	15 mm	25 mph	SE or 135°	1008 mb

[1 mark for each correctly completed column]

Pages 164–165: Glaciation

1. Boxes joined as follows:
   Ice cap – A large, thick area of ice found on land or sea in the polar regions.
   Ice sheet – Found around the edges of the polar

regions, these are thinner areas of ice.
Glacier – Forms in valleys high up in mountain ranges called alpine regions.

[2 marks if fully correct; 1 mark if one error only]

2. Any three suitable points, e.g. Snow falls in a hollow or valley [1]; this is called the zone of accumulation [1]. As more snow falls over a long period of time, it is compressed [1]; this dense snow is called firn [1] and becomes ice. Eventually the heavy ice is pulled downslope by gravity [1].

3. a) melting [1] or ablation [1]
   b) retreat   [1]
   c) snout   [1]

4. Labels added as follows:

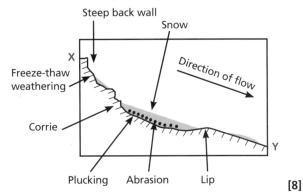

[8]

[1 mark for each correctly placed label]

5. a) Terminal [1] (i.e. at the end)
   b) Lateral [1] (i.e. on the sides)
   c) Medial [1] (i.e. in the middle)

6. Any four suitable points, e.g. An erratic is a feature of glacial deposition [1]. A piece of rock may fall onto the top of a glacier [1] or be plucked [1] from underneath or from the sides of the glacier. The glacier then transports the rock away [1] and this could be hundreds of kilometres [1]. When the glacier melts, the rock is deposited [1] in that area [1]. An erratic is a piece of rock that is usually out of character for that area [1], as in the photograph.

7. Any four suitable points, e.g. Glacial landscapes are in mountainous or hilly areas that are ideal for hikers [1], for example in the Lake District [1] in England. There are some fantastic views [1] for people to enjoy, for example at the top of Snowdon [1] in Wales. Some glacial landscapes offer ideal opportunities for leisure activities, such as climbing [1] or canoeing [1], for example the Cairngorms [1] in Scotland.

8. Any suitable problem [1] with some description [1], e.g. overcrowding; disturbing residents; congested roads; parking problems; litter; queues put visitors off; footpath erosion
   Any suitable benefit [1] with some description [1], e.g. income for local businesses; raising awareness of

the environment; money for conservation projects / improvements / better car parks; supporting local public transport

Pages 166–167: Rivers and Coasts

1. Labels completed as follows:

   1 – Tributaries [1]; 2 – Watershed [1];

   3 – Source [1]; 4 – Confluence [1];

   5 – Sea / lake [1]; 6 – Mouth [1];

   7 – Main (river) channel / Meander [1]

2.

Erosion	Hydraulic action	Abrasion	Attrition	Dissolving
	Most energy ⟵		Least energy	
Transport	Traction	Saltation	Suspension	Solution

   [1 mark each; accept 'Abrasion' and 'Attrition' in either order]

3. a) Any suitable answer. Example:

   Erosion happens on the outside of the bend where the flow is fastest [1]

   Levées [1]

   Flat land / floodplain [1]

   Inside bend [1]   Meander neck [1]   Outside bend [1]

   Deposition happens on the inside of the bend where the flow is slowest [1]

   [1 mark for each feature identified up to a maximum of 5]

   b) Any three suitable points, e.g. Erosion will continue to happen on the outside of both bends [1], which will make the meander neck narrower [1]. Eventually, that river will cut through the neck [1] and deposit sediment [1] to block off the bend and create an ox-bow lake [1].

4.

4	The circular motion causes small waves that move forward in the direction of the wind.
1	The Sun's energy causes variation in air temperature, which causes wind as warm air rises and cooler air fills its place.
3	The friction causes a circular motion to start in the water.
6	The top of the wave moves faster than the bottom, causing the wave to break.
5	When the wave reaches the coast, the friction of the sea floor causes the wave to increase in height.
2	The wind blows over the surface of the sea, which causes friction.

   [3 marks if fully correct; 2 marks if one error only; 1 mark if two errors only]

5. a) Any three suitable points, e.g. Harder rock, for example chalk [1], will be more resistant [1]

to erosion. This means it will take longer for landforms to be created [1] or for cliff retreat to occur [1]. Softer rock, for example sand/clay [1], will erode more quickly [1] and cause the coast to retreat [1]. Rates of erosion will be much higher with softer rock [1].

   b) Any three suitable points, e.g. The longer the fetch, the greater the distance the wind can blow across the sea [1]. The longer the distance the wind can blow across the sea, the greater the energy of the waves [1]. Waves with more energy are likely to mean higher rates of erosion [1]. The longer the fetch, the more erosion [1]. An example of a long fetch is the west coast of the UK [1]. An example of a short fetch is the east coast of the UK [1].

   c) Any three suitable points, e.g. Destructive waves will cause more erosion than constructive waves [1]. Constructive waves will push sediment up a beach [1], creating a wider beach that means fewer waves reach the cliff [1]. Destructive waves will attack a headland and erode it [1]. They will also remove sediment from a beach [1], meaning that the waves can reach the cliff [1].

6. Any suitable written explanation (up to 6 marks) supported by a diagram (up to 2 marks), e.g.

   1 – Weaknesses (cracks/joints) in the rock are eroded [1] by hydraulic action [1].

   2 – The cracks are widened to become caves [1].

   3 – As the caves are eroded from both sides of the headland [1], they meet in the middle to form an arch [1].

   4 – The roof of the arch is weathered [1] and collapses to leave a stack [1].

   5 – Over time, the stack is eroded and weathered down to leave a stump [1].

Pages 168–169: Landscapes

1. **Any suitable answers, e.g.**

Use	Benefit	Drawback
Removal of trees to make space for human activity	New space to build houses [1] New space for farming [1]	Destroys natural habitats for animals [1] Increases CO_2 levels by removing trees [1]
Extracting minerals and rocks from mines and quarries	Provides raw materials to for manufacturing [1] Contributes to a country's income [1]	Creates pollution due to heavy machinery for mining [1] The environment may be destroyed so that mines and quarries can be developed [1]
Extracting water from rivers and underground stores	Water can be used for irrigating crops during periods of drought [1] Water can be used for industry, e.g. washing and cooling things [1] Water available to meet growing domestic demand [1]	Stores of water are being used up faster than they are being recharged (replaced) [1] Water may be returned to the water cycle with toxic chemicals in it [1]
Using fossil fuels to provide energy	Humans can benefit from cheap and accessible transport [1] Jobs are created in the energy production process [1]	Burning fossil fuels contributes to climate change [1] Fossil fuels are a finite resource and may run out [1]

[1 mark maximum for each completed cell]

2. **Any suitable definition and example, e.g.** Carrying capacity refers to the maximum number of people that an area can support [1] by them being able to grow enough food [1]. Any desert area [1] would have a low carrying capacity (as the soil is infertile).

3. **Any two suitable points, e.g.** Some country's rainforests cover huge areas [1] that would be too big to monitor in any other way [1]. Images can be easily taken at regular intervals to check if deforestation is happening [1]. Sending police / government officials to monitor the forests is risky as some of the illegal loggers can be dangerous [1].

[2 marks maximum]

4.

Statement	Tick if correct
Carbon-neutral companies do not produce any carbon at all.	
Carbon-neutral companies use strategies to reduce their carbon emissions.	✓
Trees may be planted to absorb carbon dioxide to offset a company's carbon emissions.	✓
Carbon-neutral companies always put profit before the environment.	
Some people think some carbon-neutral companies are not telling the truth.	✓

[2 marks if fully correct; 1 mark if one error only]

5. More sustainable: B **[1]**
   Any two suitable points by way of explanation, e.g. The field in photograph A has been ploughed down the slope [1]; the field in B has been ploughed across the slope [1]. When it rains, the soil in photograph A is more likely to be eroded than the soil in B [1]. The technique in photograph B is called 'contour ploughing' [1]. **[2 marks maximum]**

6. a) **Any suitable description, e.g.** A tribesman is selling traditional items [1] that he and his tribe have made; this could be for tourists to buy as souvenirs [1]. **[2 marks maximum]**
   Any suitable benefit, e.g. This can provide some income to Maasai people [1], so they can use the money to buy things [1], and potentially upgrade their traditional methods [1]. **[1 mark maximum]**
   Any suitable drawback, e.g. This erodes their traditional way of life [1] and the Maasai may be exploited by travel companies and tourists [1]. **[1 mark maximum]**

   b) **Any suitable description, e.g.** The Makoro tribesman is taking tourists on a trip on a traditional logboat [1]. This is an example of eco-tourism, where sustainability is important [1]. **[2 marks maximum]**
   Any suitable benefit, e.g. Makoro people who work in the tourism industry do not get attracted to work in illegal logging [1]; they can get a good income from tourism [1]. Eco-tourism raises awareness of fragile environments [1]. **[1 mark maximum]**
   Any suitable drawback, e.g. Eco-tourists have to fly to their destination, which causes carbon emissions [1]. Some tourism companies may take advantage of the Makoro and pay them poor wages [1]. **[1 mark maximum]**

Pages 170–179 **Human Geography**

Pages 170–171: Population

1.

Statement	Tick if correct
Between 1750 and 1950, the world population grew very rapidly.	
Since 1950, the world population has grown very rapidly.	✓
By 2050, the world population will be more than 15 billion people.	
The population has grown faster in the poorer countries than the richer countries.	✓
Since 2000, the world population has started to decrease.	
The world population in 2020 was approximately 7.9 billion people.	✓
By 2050, there will be more people living in richer countries than in poorer countries.	
World population grew faster from 1950–2000 than from 1850–1900.	✓

[2 marks if fully correct; 1 mark if one error only]

2. **Any suitable answers, e.g.**
   a) UK; The Netherlands; India; Bangladesh; Nigeria **[2]**
   b) Australia; Russia; Greenland; Canada **[2]**
3. The number of people that live in an area **[1]**
4. **Any four suitable points, e.g.** Some parts of the world have natural resources [1], such as USA with oil and gas [1]. Flat land [1] makes it easy for

settlements to be built **[1]**. Countries like France have fertile soils **[1]** and this is good for farming **[1]**. Countries such as the UK have a moderate climate **[1]** with no extremes in temperature or rainfall **[1]**.

5. **Boxes joined as follows:**
    The process of people moving into a country – Immigration **[1]**
    People who move to a country for jobs and higher wages – Economic migrants **[1]**
    People fleeing conflict or persecution – Refugees **[1]**

6. **Any two suitable points, e.g.** Lack of family planning or contraception **[1]**; religious beliefs **[1]**; high rates of infant mortality **[1]**; want lots of children to help with farming **[1]**; low status of women in society **[1]**

7. **Any suitable points, e.g.**
    Advantages: people will volunteer with community events **[1]**; help with childcare **[1]**; lower levels of crime **[1]**; pass on experience and knowledge to younger generations **[1]**   **[2 marks maximum]**
    Disadvantages: lack of people of a working age to fill jobs **[1]**; high demand for medical care **[1]**; financial cost to government of pension costs **[1]**; high demand for specialist housing **[1]**
    [2 marks maximum]

Pages 172–173: Urbanisation

1.

Key term	Definition
Counterurbanisation	People move from cities to surrounding smaller towns and villages
Urbanisation	Increasing proportions of people living in towns and cities
Suburbanisation	People moving outwards within a city, causing the city to grow

[2 marks if fully correct; 1 mark if one correct]

2.
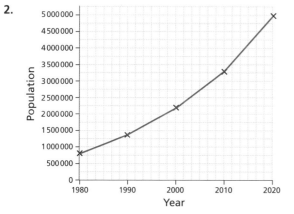
[2 marks for correctly plotted data; 1 mark if one error]

3. A city with a population over 10 million   **[1]**

4. **Any four suitable points, e.g.** Birth rates are higher than death rates **[1]**, leading to natural increase **[1]**. Rural-to-urban migration **[1]**, where people move from rural areas to urban areas **[1]**. Push factors encourage people to leave rural areas **[1]**, such as flooding **[1]**, inadequate healthcare provision **[1]** and lack of job opportunities **[1]**. Pull factors attract people to live in cities **[1]**, such as jobs **[1]**, higher wages **[1]** and better access to electricity and water supply **[1]**.

5. a) **Any three suitable labels, e.g.**
    High density **[1]**; makeshift housing **[1]**; rubbish in streets **[1]**; unpaved road/paths **[1]**; unwanted land **[1]**; no structure/planning **[1]**

    b) **Any suitable effect, e.g.**
    High density – lack of privacy **[1]**; disease spreads quickly **[1]**, which means people can't work **[1]**. Rubbish in streets – looks unsightly **[1]**; might attract flies or rats **[1]**, leading to spread of disease **[1]**. Makeshift housing – vulnerable to collapse in high winds or rain **[1]**; cold for people at night **[1]**; unhealthy living conditions **[1]**

6. **Any suitable points, e.g.**

Feature of city	How it can be made more sustainable
Housing	Loft insulation **[1]**; double/triple glazed windows **[1]**; solar panels on roofs **[1]**
Transport	Cycle lanes **[1]**; provision of public transport **[1]**; car sharing **[1]**; pedestrianising streets **[1]**
Waste	Recycling **[1]**; reduced consumption **[1]**; composting food waste **[1]**

[1 mark for one suitable point in each row]

Pages 174–175: Development

1.

Key term	Definition
Infant mortality **[1]**	The number of children that die before they reach their first birthday per 1000 live births per year
Gross domestic product **[1]**	The total value of goods and services produced by a country per year
Adult literacy **[1]**	The percentage of people over 15 that can read and write

2. **Any suitable definition, e.g.** Economic and social wellbeing **[1]**; quality of life / standard of living **[1]**; how well people live **[1]**

3. **Any two suitable points, e.g.** It can be misleading **[1]**. For example, some countries have a high gross domestic product, but this wealth is in the hands of only a few people **[1]**.

4. **Any two suitable points, e.g.** They are mainly in the Northern Hemisphere **[1]**; North America **[1]**; many are European countries **[1]**; also found in Oceania / Australia and New Zealand **[1]**

5. **Any four suitable points, e.g.** Natural disasters mean that money is spent on recovery, not development **[1]**; some countries are landlocked, which makes trade difficult **[1]**; debts need to be paid off, which limits the money available for development **[1]**; corrupt governments mean that money is not used to develop health, education and other services **[1]**; exports are lower in value than imports, leading to a trade deficit **[1]**; past colonial activities stripped many low income countries of their resources **[1]**

6.

Where the money goes	Percentage
Country of coffee growth	25 [1]
Transport company	7
Country of coffee company head office	68 [1]

7.

Statement	Tick if correct
Producers receive a price that gives a reasonable profit.	✓ [1]
Producers get paid the lowest price possible.	
Producers sell their products at a cheap price.	

8. Any suitable points, e.g.
    Advantages: improved access to water [1]; reduces illness/disease [1]; creates jobs [1]; improves people's skills [1]; improves access to energy [1]; provides people with emergency shelter [1]   **[2 marks maximum]**
    Disadvantages: conditions may be attached [1]; can lead to negative environmental impacts [1]; corrupt governments mean that the aid does not go to where it is needed [1]; can lead to dependency on the donor country [1]; can lead to debt [1]
    [2 marks maximum]

Pages 176–177: Economic Activity

1.

Primary	Secondary	Tertiary	Quaternary
Farmer	Baker	Nurse	IT consultant
	Builder	Accountant	

[1 mark for each correctly completed column]

2. Any suitable answer, e.g.

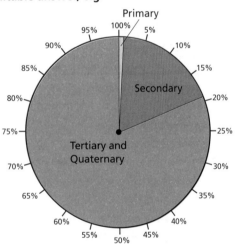

**[1 mark for correctly plotted data;
1 mark for correct labelling]**

3. **Any suitable difference, e.g.** Higher percentage of people employed in the primary sector in Kenya compared to the UK [1]; lower percentage of people employed in the tertiary and quaternary sectors in Kenya compared to the UK [1].

4. **Any four suitable points, e.g.** Some foods cannot be grown in the UK [1], such as bananas and rice [1]. This is because of the climate [1]. Some seasonal foods, such as strawberries [1], must be imported at certain times of year because the weather is not suitable to grow these crops [1]. It is cheaper to import them than grow them in the UK [1]. There is demand for exotic food that cannot be grown in the UK [1], such as pomegranates [1].

5. **Any suitable definition, e.g.** Not using chemicals [1]; not using fertilisers/pesticides [1]

6. Manufacturing mainly used to take place in **HICs**, such as the UK and USA. A lot of manufacturing now occurs in **LICs** and **NICs**, such as China, Brazil and Mexico. In these countries, labour costs are **lower**, land is often cheaper and environmental laws are **less** strict.   **[1 mark each]**

7. **Any two suitable points, e.g.** Wages are low [1]; poor working conditions [1]; long working hours [1]; female workers' rights are being overlooked [1]

8.

Statement	Tick if correct
Tertiary and quaternary sector jobs are the main type of job in HICs.	✓
All tertiary and quaternary sector jobs are very highly paid.	
In HICs, the number of people working in the tertiary and quaternary sectors has decreased over time.	
There are a wide range of different types of tertiary and quaternary jobs.	✓

[2 marks if fully correct; 1 mark if one error only]

Pages 178–179: Natural Resources

1.

Non-renewable	Renewable
Oil	Solar energy
Iron ore	Wood

[2 marks if fully correct; 1 mark if one error only]

2. **Any suitable definition, e.g.** Meeting the needs of today's people without compromising future generations   **[1]**

3. **Any two suitable points, e.g.** Recycling [1]; using smaller quantities [1]; using resources more efficiently [1]; exploiting undeveloped resources [1]; finding alternative non-renewable sources [1]

4. **Any suitable points, e.g.**
    Advantages: creates jobs [1]; earns money [1]; boosts exports/trade [1]; provides resources [1], such as wood for construction [1]   **[2 marks maximum]**
    Disadvantages: destroys habitats [1]; affects wildlife / food chains [1]; leads to soil erosion [1]; there will be more carbon dioxide in the air [1], causing climate change [1]   **[2 marks maximum]**

5. **Any suitable sentences, e.g.**
    Overfishing is catching too many fish so there are not enough to breed naturally   **[1]**
    Fish farms are a place where fish are artificially bred and grown for human use   **[1]**

6.

Statement	Tick if correct
Gas is the main type of fuel used to create electricity.	✓
Nuclear was used more than wind and solar in 2020 to create electricity.	
In 2020, oil was the most used fuel to create electricity.	
Between 2000 and 2020, the amount of electricity created by hydro doubled.	
The amount of coal used to create electricity rapidly decreased from 2000 to 2020.	✓
Renewable energy as a source of electricity increased between 2000 and 2020.	✓

[2 marks if fully correct; 1 mark if one error only]

7. **Any four suitable points, e.g.** Coal is being phased out as it causes air pollution **[1]**; coal releases greenhouses gases like carbon dioxide **[1]**, which contributes to climate change **[1]**. The UK government wants to reduce the use of fossil fuels **[1]** to meet targets set by international agreements **[1]**. Smaller quantities of fossil fuel are being used because supplies in the UK are slowly running out **[1]**. Renewable types of energy are being developed as they will last forever **[1]** and they don't release any pollutants **[1]**. The UK is developing wind energy due to favourable climate conditions **[1]**. There are lots of suitable sites for wind turbines, both offshore **[1]** and on land in hilly/mountainous areas **[1]**.

Pages 180–185 Geography Skills

Pages 180–181: Ordnance Survey Maps

1. **Any five suitable pieces of evidence, e.g.** hotel **[1]**; sea life sanctuary **[1]**; leisure centre **[1]**; sensory park **[1]**; caravan/camping site **[1]**; tourist information **[1]**; car park **[1]**; beach **[1]**; public toilets **[1]**; surfing activities **[1]**

2. North east **[1]**

3. South west **[1]**

4. Hunstanton Park **[1]**

5. 7040 **[1]**

6. Mill Farm **[1]**

7. 671391 **[1]**

8. A reservoir **[1]**

9. 705448 **[1]**

10. Fairly flat **[1]**; low lying **[1]**

11. 52 m **[1]**

12. 5 m **[1]**

13. Between 300 and 400 m **[1]**

14. Between 3.5 and 4 km **[1]**

15. Between 5 and 5.5 km **[1]**

Pages 182–183: Geographic Information Systems

1.

Statement	Tick if correct
Geographic Information Systems are online textbooks providing descriptions and explanations of key geographical concepts.	
Computer hardware, software and digital data is used to create maps.	✓
Data can be changed, analysed and viewed in different ways to see geographical patterns and relationships.	✓
Data is sorted out so it can be displayed using various graphical techniques.	
Maps are drawn by hand to show the layout of places.	
Geographic Information Systems can be accessed using a computer or a tablet.	✓
Geographic Information Systems use layers of information stacked on top of each other.	✓
Spreadsheets are a good example of Geographic Information Systems.	

[2 marks if fully correct; 1 mark if one error only]

2. **Any two suitable examples and reasons, e.g.**
Police **[1]**: to plot crime patterns **[1]**; to identify areas that need crime prevention **[1]**
Ambulance service **[1]**: to identify locations of ambulances **[1]**; to identify which ambulance is best located to respond to an emergency call **[1]**
Water / gas / electricity companies **[1]**: to map the position of underground pipes and cables **[1]**; to record the condition of pipes and cables **[1]**
Supermarkets **[1]**: to plan deliveries **[1]**
Delivery companies **[1]**: to plan the quickest routes for deliveries **[1]** **[1 mark for each example; 1 mark for an accompanying reason]**

3. **Any two suitable answers, e.g.** contour lines **[1]**; numbers show the height of the land in metres **[1]**; triangulation points mark the top of hills/mountains **[1]**; spot heights **[1]**

4. **Boxes joined as follows:**
Points – Symbols that represent a feature at a particular location
Lines – Symbols that show things such as rivers and roads
Polygons – Shapes to show things such as buildings, lakes and forests
Text – Used for the names of places or landscape features **[2 marks if fully correct; 1 mark if one error only]**

5. **Any suitable definition, e.g.** technology that uses georeferenced data to create maps **[1]**; online maps that show data specific to a location **[1]**

6. **Any two suitable points, e.g.** a virtual globe **[1]**; maps, satellite images and aerial photographs **[1]**; maps with different layers of data **[1]**; enables you to see locations at different scales **[1]**; shows live data such as weather **[1]**; enables you to see how a place has changed over time **[1]**

7. A: Satellite image   B: Aerial photograph **[1]**

8. **Any suitable point, e.g.** You can see if deforestation has occurred in a given length of time **[1]**; you can see how much deforestation has occurred in a given length of time **[1]**

Pages 184–185: Fieldwork

1.

Stage of geography fieldwork	Rank order (1 = first, 6 = last)
Collecting data	2
Displaying data	3
Setting a question/hypothesis	1
Drawing conclusions	6
Collating data	4
Analysing data	5

[2 marks if fully correct; 1 mark if one error only]

2. a)

Type of sampling	Tick if correct
Random	
Stratified	
Systematic	✓ **[1]**
Opportunity sampling	

   b) **Any two suitable points, e.g.** It might be difficult to get to **[1]** because the land may be very steep **[1]**. The land might be private land **[1]** so not accessible to the public **[1]**. There may be animals in the area **[1]** so it would be dangerous **[1]**.

3. **Any two suitable points, e.g.** ask a greater number of people **[1]**; provide options for people to choose from **[1]**; question 4 is not directly relevant to the aim of the questionnaire **[1]**; there is no question about how long people are staying for **[1]**.

4. a) **Any suitable answer, e.g.** scatter graph **[1]**; bar chart **[1]**

   b) **Any suitable answer, e.g.** river depth **[1]**; river speed/velocity **[1]**; size of bedload **[1]**; land use **[1]**

   c) **Any two suitable points, e.g.** There is a positive correlation **[1]**, as distance down the river increases the width increases **[1]**; there is an anomaly at location F **[1]**, where the river is narrower than expected **[1]**

5. a)

   [1 mark for each row]

   b) **Any suitable answer, e.g.** bar chart **[1]**; pie chart **[1]**; divided bar graph **[1]**; radar diagram **[1]**

   c) **Any suitable answer, e.g.** effective for percentage data **[1]**; visual so you can see patterns **[1]**; easy to compare between different types of transport **[1]**

   d) **Any suitable answer, e.g.** car is the most popular type of transport **[1]**; bus is the least popular type of transport **[1]**

Pages 186–202: Mixed Test-Style Questions

1. **Any four suitable points, e.g.** The population of a country will grow **[1]** if the birth rate is higher than the death rate **[1]**; this is called natural increase **[1]**. When immigration is higher than emigration **[1]**, there will be an increase in population **[1]**.

2. **Any two suitable points, e.g.** Good availability of contraception **[1]**; higher levels of education **[1]**; children are expensive to bring up **[1]**; more desire for material possessions than a large family **[1]**; later age of marriage **[1]**; more women having careers **[1]**

3. a) Europe **[1]**; Asia **[1]**

   b) **Any four from:** Norway; Finland; Estonia; Latvia; Lithuania; Poland; Belarus; Ukraine; Georgia; Azerbaijan; Kazakhstan; China; Mongolia; North Korea; South Ossetia; Abkhazia **[1 mark each]**

4. **Any two suitable points, e.g.** The Chinese government was worried about overpopulation **[1]**, which would have put a lot of pressure on resources **[1]** such as food/water/energy **[1]**. Only allowing one child per family would slow population growth **[1]**.

5. a) 2030 **[1]**

   b) 1.53 billion **[1]**

6.

Statement	Tick if correct
Scientists can accurately predict when volcanoes are going to erupt and usually evacuate people to safety.	✓
Volcanoes cause fires but earthquakes do not.	
It is easy to protect people and buildings from the hot lava and ash from a volcanic eruption.	
It is almost impossible to predict exactly when an earthquake will happen.	✓
Land is being destroyed as it melts owing to the magma rising up through the plate margin.	

   [2 marks if fully correct; 1 mark if one error only]

7. **Any two suitable points, e.g.** more open space **[1]**; lower levels of air pollution **[1]**; lower noise levels **[1]**; community spirit **[1]**; attractive area in which to live **[1]**

8. **Any four suitable points, e.g.** Increased house prices **[1]**; increased traffic on local roads **[1]**; increased levels of air pollution **[1]**; building houses destroys greenfield sites / areas of open space **[1]**; conflict between existing residents and new residents **[1]**; new buildings don't fit in with the old buildings **[1]**

9. **Any three suitable points, e.g.** Weather satellites take (high definition) photographs **[1]** that are used by scientists to observe what is happening in the atmosphere **[1]**. Satellite images can show cloud cover **[1]** and even where it is raining **[1]**. Forecasters can look at sequences of images over time **[1]**, which

can help with predicting how the weather will behave next [1].

10. a) **Any three suitable points, e.g.** The Suez Canal joins the Mediterranean and the Indian Ocean, which makes the transport of goods between some countries much shorter [1] than going around the southern tip of Africa [1]. It means that companies spend less money [1] on transporting their products and they can operate more quickly [1].

   b) **Any two suitable points, e.g.** Ships transporting goods around the world can have shorter journeys [1], meaning that they burn far less (fossil) fuel, which in turn reduces the impact on global warming [1].

11. **Any two suitable points, e.g.** The photograph shows nomadic pastoralism [1]. This involves farmers moving their animals around [1] to find food and water [1].

12. **Any suitable example in each row.** **[1 mark for each]**

Type of country	Named example
High income country (HIC)	UK; USA; France; Japan; Australia
Newly industrialising country (NIC)	China; India; Brazil; Mexico; South Africa
Low income country (LIC)	Kenya; Sudan; Ethiopia; Mali; Uganda

13. **Any three suitable points, e.g.** The Human Development Index is a composite indicator [1]. It measures several development indicators [1], such as life expectancy, adult literacy and GDP per capita [1]. This is fair [1] because several factors are considered rather than just one [1]. The closer the Human Development Index is to 1, the more developed a country is [1].

14.

Statement	Tick if correct
As the standard of living in the UK has increased, more people have been employed in secondary activities.	
Over 70% of people work in the tertiary and quaternary sectors.	✓
The number of people employed in primary activities has decreased due to the population of the UK falling.	
Machines do a lot of the work in primary and secondary activities, meaning that fewer people work in these types of jobs.	✓

[2 marks if fully correct; 1 mark if one error only]

15. **Any two suitable points, plus one example, e.g.** Indigenous people are those who have lived in a certain place for a very long time [1], perhaps thousands of years. Examples are the Yanomamo from the Amazon [1] or the Maasai in Kenya [1]. They may live a traditional lifestyle [1] and get their resources from the surrounding area [1], such as food, medicine and clothes [1].

16. **Any three suitable points, e.g.** As the world's urban areas expand and our needs for space grow [1], we are moving closer and into the areas where indigenous people live [1]. Land may be cleared for extensive farming [1]; for cattle / soya / palm oil [1]; for resource extraction [1]; for oil / gold exploitation [1]. Global warming is affecting the ability of some indigenous people to get what they need from the area in which they live [1]. For these reasons, indigenous people can be forced to move away [1], losing their traditional way of life and moving to modern society [1].

17. **Any three suitable points, e.g.** 1953 was the end of the civil war in Korea [1]. A new leader took over the government and made a lot of changes [1]. Some of the changes were better transport infrastructure [1], the government supporting manufacturing industry [1] and building more schools to improve education [1].

18. Ordered longest to shortest: Eons; Eras; Periods **[1]**
   Example of a Period: Quaternary; Tertiary; Cretaceous; Jurassic; Triassic; Permian; Carboniferous; Devonian; Silurian; Ordovician; Cambrian; Precambrian **[1 mark for any example]**
   Example of an Eon: Phanerozoic; Proterozoic; Archean; Hadean **[1 mark for any example]**
   Example of an Era: Cenozoic; Mesozoic; Palaeozoic **[1 mark for any example]**

19. **Any three suitable points, e.g.** Scientists think global warming is increasing owing to human activity (enhanced greenhouse effect) [1]. Increasing temperatures mean more areas of the world are becoming much hotter [1]. More water is evaporating from the oceans [1] and this means there is more precipitation [1], leading to more floods [1].

20. **Any four suitable points, e.g.** cheaper labour [1]; cheaper land [1]; more relaxed environmental regulations [1]; more relaxed labour laws [1]; large population centres mean lots of potential workers are available [1]; the country has access to the ocean for shipping goods and materials [1]

21. **These options should be circled:** deciduous [1]; hardwood [1]; oak [1]; slow growing [1]

22. a) Agriculture [1]; primary [1]
   b) Tourism [1]; tertiary [1]
   c) Making souvenirs from lava [1]; secondary [1]

23. **Any three suitable points, e.g.** Gas is the most used energy source in the UK [1]. North Sea gas is running out [1], so gas must be imported [1]. If the UK did not import gas, there might be energy shortages [1].

24. **Any two suitable points, e.g.** spot heights [1]; contours [1]; triangulation points [1]

25. GIS stands for **Geographic** Information System. This involves using **layers** of information so that data can be **presented** and analysed for different locations. This enables **patterns** and relationships to be identified. **[1 mark for each]**

26. **Any two suitable points, e.g.** Delivery addresses can be identified on a map [1]. The quickest route

can be plotted [1], reducing costs [1] and increasing efficiency / saving time [1].

27. a) **Any five suitable points, e.g.** Formed when heat and pressure cause rocks to change. [1]. Tectonic movements [1] cause rocks to get closer to the hot magma [1]. Heat changes the chemicals in the rocks [1]. Minerals are arranged in layers [1].

   b) **Any four suitable points, e.g.** The slate is non-porous [1] so rainwater can run off the surface easily [1]. It is less susceptible to weathering [1] and so will last a long time [1]. It forms in layers [1], which makes it easy to cut into tiles [1].

28. **Any three suitable points, e.g.** Volcanoes may provide opportunities for economic activities [1]. Fertile soils mean that the land around a volcano might be good for growing crops [1] to provide food for people to eat [1] or export to other countries [1].
   Or
   Tourists may come to see the volcanic landscape / activity [1], which means that they will spend money in the area [1], contributing to the economy [1]. Tourism means that there will be jobs for local people [1].

29. **Any suitable answers, e.g.**

   a) Oceanic crust is thinner than continental crust [1]. Oceanic crust is under the ocean, whereas continental crust is land based [1]. Oceanic crust is made of basalt, but continental crust is made of granite / they are different rock types [1].

   b) The Earth's inner core is solid (metal), but the mantle is molten (rock) [1]. The inner core is hotter than the mantle [1].

   c) Plates move towards each other at a destructive plate margin but away from each other at a constructive plate margin [1]. New land is created at a constructive plate margin but destroyed at a destructive plate margin [1].

   d) The focus of the earthquake is where the shockwaves start, and the epicentre is where they reach the surface [1]. The focus is (usually) underground, and the epicentre is on the surface directly above the focus [1].

   e) A shield volcano has gently sloping sides, whereas a composite one has steeper sides [1]. The lava in a shield volcano is usually runny (less viscous) whereas in a composite one it is thicker (more viscous) [1]. A shield volcano has a wide base whereas a composite one is narrower [1].

   f) An active volcano is one which is erupting, or has erupted recently, whereas a dormant one has erupted in the past but a long time ago (and it could still erupt in the future) [1].

   [1 mark maximum for each part]

30. **Any four suitable answers, e.g.**

	Closed question	Open question
Advantage	Easy to fill in [1] Data is organised into categories [1] Easy to turn data into graphs [1]	Can get well detailed answers [1] Allows people to express their opinion [1]
Disadvantage	Answer might not fit a category [1] Answer lacks detail [1]	Answer might be brief or don't know [1] Takes longer to record [1] Difficult to present the data in graphs [1]

31. **Any two suitable answers, e.g.** Questionnaire [1]; environmental quality survey [1]; photographs/ sketches [1]; traffic counts [1]; pedestrian counts [1]; air pollution measurements [1]; land use survey [1]; litter count [1]; noise measurements [1]

32. **Any four suitable points, e.g.** The physical weathering process is freeze-thaw / frost shattering [1]. Water has entered the cracks in the rock (chalk) [1] and the temperature has fluctuated above and below 0°C [1], which means that the water has frozen [1], widening any cracks [1]. The water then melts [1] and runs further into the crack it has widened and the process repeats [1]. Eventually, there are so many cracks in the rock that the front of the cliff face falls down [1].

33. **Any three suitable points, e.g.** Rock is heated by the sun, and then cools again [1], and this process is repeated [1]. As the outer layers of the rock expand and contract [1], they become loose from the layers underneath [1] and they peel off like the layers of an onion [1].

34. **Any two suitable points, e.g.** The limpets ingest particles of the rock that they are living on [1]. As the limpets move around, their shells may wear the rock away by scraping it [1].

35. **Labels and graphs joined as follows:**

   a) Savannah – A; Desert – B; Monsoon – C; Equatorial – D   **[2]**
   [1 mark if one error only]

   b) Mediterranean – E; Polar – F; Tundra – G; Steppe – H   **[2]**
   [1 mark if one error only]

36. a) North east   [1]
   b) Llyn y Gadair   [1]
   c) Between 375 and 525 m   [1]
   d) Yes   [1]
   e) i) Corrie   [1]
      ii) **Any three suitable points, e.g.** Contour lines are close together / very steep [1]; contour lines in a crescent shape suggests armchair-shaped landform [1]; small round lake in the bottom [1]
   f) 715124   [1]
   g) 893 m   [1]

37. Table completed as follows (the order in each column is not important):

Coasts	Fluvial	Glacial
Hydraulic action	Hydraulic action	Plucking
Stump	Meander	Meltwater
Longshore drift	Slip-off slope (point – bar)	Moraine
Suspension	Suspension	Suspension
Traction	Traction	Steep back wall
Fetch	Floodplain	Lip

[1 mark for each correctly completed column; 'Traction' could also be correctly included in the Glacial column]

38. a) **Any four suitable points, e.g.** Energy from the sun (insolation) [1] is more concentrated near to the Equator [1] as the sun is directly overhead [1]. Towards the poles, the angle of the sun's rays is lower [1] and so the energy is spread out over a larger area [1].

b) **Suitable labels could include the following six points:** North facing (left end of the arrow) [1]; south facing (right end of the arrow) [1]; on the north-facing side, because there is a shadow from the mountain behind / the slope is facing away from the sun [1], the temperature is cold enough to allow snow to accumulate [1]. On the slope with an aspect to the south, the sun melts any snow [1] so that it does not get chance to accumulate enough to become firn [1].

c) **Any two suitable points, e.g.** Alpine environments are cold enough for snow to accumulate [1] because of the altitude [1] and owing to the temperature decreasing by approximately 1°C per 100 m increase in height [1].

39. a) **Any two suitable points, e.g.** Attrition [1] is the action of sediment knocking into other sediment [1], so it only changes the size and shape of the sediment itself [1].

b) **Any two suitable points, e.g.** The size of sediment can affect the angle of a beach's slope [1]. Smaller sediment, for example sand, tends to form shallower slopes/gradients [1], whereas larger sediment tends to form steeper gradients [1]. There is a link between attrition and the slope of the beach [1].

40. a) A choropleth map [1]

b) i) Area A [1]

ii) The choropleth map uses categories so we only know that there were 0–20 visitors. [1]

41. Any suitable point for each benefit and drawback, e.g.
Maasai tribespeople
One of the benefits could be…
that we can sell souvenirs to earn money [1]; that we can be safari guides [1]; that it might raise awareness of our way of life [1].
One of the drawbacks could be…
that our traditional way of life could be put at risk [1]; that we don't want lots of people disturbing us [1]; that it could change where we can live [1]

A hotel manager in Mombasa
One of the benefits could be…
that we will have more income from tourists [1]; that we can provide more jobs for local people [1].
One of the drawbacks could be…
that the hotel may have to pay the travel agent more money [1]; that the numbers of expected tourists could fall for sudden reasons (such as a pandemic) and the costs of running the hotel would still remain [1].

An environmentalist
One of the benefits could be…
that people's awareness of the environment could be raised [1]; that it will bring income for environmental projects [1]; that we have more control over where people go and what they do [1].
One of the drawbacks could be…
that people will need to fly to get there, which contributes to global warming [1]; that habitats could be damaged to make way for hotels and roads [1]; that animals might be disturbed [1].

42. **Any four suitable points, e.g.** The local resident would most likely want the most effective flood defences in place [1], which would usually be hard engineering such as flood diversion channels [1] / artificial levées [1] / dams [1]. An environmentalist is likely to prefer soft engineering methods, such as afforestation [1] / channel dredging [1], as these work with nature [1] and do not disturb ecosystems [1] in the way that hard engineering does.

Acknowledgements

The authors and publisher are grateful to the copyright holders for permission to use quoted materials and images.

Page 164: GeoJuice / Alamy Stock Photo

Page 166: Matjaz Corel / Alamy Stock Photo

Page 169: BIOSPHOTO / Alamy Stock Photo; lemanieh / Alamy Stock Photo; Alissa Everett / Alamy Stock Photo; GFC Collection / Alamy Stock Photo

Page 173: John Cancalosi / Alamy Stock Photo

Page 174: Source: United Nations Development Programme, Human Development Report 2020 OurWorldInData.org/human-development-index/ • CC BY

Page 179: Data sourced from https://www.gov.uk/government/statistics/uk-in-energy-brief-2021

Page 183: Claudia Weinmann / Alamy Stock Photo; Aleksandr Vorobev / Alamy Stock Photo

Page 188: A.P.S. (UK) / Alamy Stock Photo

Page 192: Derek Croucher / Alamy Stock Photo

Page 193: Hiren Ranpara / Alamy Stock Photo

All other images are © Shutterstock.com

This product uses map data licensed from Ordnance Survey® with the permission of the Controller of HMSO. © Crown copyright. License number 100018598.

Every effort has been made to trace copyright holders and obtain their permission for the use of copyright material. The authors and publisher will gladly receive information enabling them to rectify any error or omission in subsequent editions. All facts are correct at time of going to press.

Published by Collins

An imprint of HarperCollins*Publishers*

1 London Bridge Street

London SE1 9GF

HarperCollins*Publishers*

Macken House, 39/40 Mayor Street Upper, Dublin 1, D01 C9W8, Ireland

© HarperCollins*Publishers* Limited 2023

ISBN 9780008551483

First published 2023

10 9 8 7 6 5 4 3

British Library Cataloguing in Publication Data.

A CIP record of this book is available from the British Library.

Publisher: Clare Souza

Commissioning and Editorial: Richard Toms

Authors: David Rayner, Andrew Browne, Victoria Turner, Alison Farrell, Adam Gibson and Tony Grundy

Videos: Eleanor Barker

Cover Design: Kevin Robbins and Sarah Duxbury

Inside Concept Design: Sarah Duxbury and Paul Oates

Text Design and Layout: Jouve India Private Limited and Nicola Lancashire (Rose and Thorn Creative Services)

Production: Emma Wood

Printed in the United Kingdom by Martins the Printers

This book is produced from independently certified FSC™ paper to ensure responsible forest management.

For more information visit: www.harpercollins.co.uk/green